T0114133

Cambridge Elements ≡

Elements in Publishing and Book Culture
edited by
Samantha Rayner
University College London

AFRICAN LITERATURE AND THE CIA

Networks of Authorship and Publishing

Caroline Davis
Oxford Brookes University

CAMBRIDGE
UNIVERSITY PRESS

CAMBRIDGE
UNIVERSITY PRESS

University Printing House, Cambridge CB2 8BS, United Kingdom

One Liberty Plaza, 20th Floor, New York, NY 10006, USA

477 Williamstown Road, Port Melbourne, VIC 3207, Australia

314–321, 3rd Floor, Plot 3, Splendor Forum, Jasola District Centre,
New Delhi – 110025, India

79 Anson Road, #06–04/06, Singapore 079906

Cambridge University Press is part of the University of Cambridge.

It furthers the University's mission by disseminating knowledge in the pursuit of
education, learning, and research at the highest international levels of excellence.

www.cambridge.org
Information on this title: www.cambridge.org/9781108725545
DOI: 10.1017/9781108663229

First published 2020

A catalogue record for this publication is available from the British Library.

ISBN 978-1-108-72554-5 Paperback
ISSN 2514-8524 (online)
ISSN 2514-8516 (print)

African Literature and the CIA

Networks of Authorship and Publishing

Elements in Publishing and Book Culture

DOI: 10.1017/9781108663229

First published online: December 2020

Caroline Davis

Oxford Brookes University

Author for correspondence: Caroline Davis, cdavis@brookes.ac.uk

ABSTRACT: During the period of decolonisation in Africa, the CIA covertly subsidised a number of African authors, editors and publishers as part of its anti-communist propaganda strategy. Managed by two front organisations, the Congress of Cultural Freedom and the Farfield Foundation, its Africa programme stretched across the continent. This Element unravels the hidden networks and associations underpinning African literary publishing in the 1960s; it evaluates the success of the CIA in secretly infiltrating and influencing African literary magazines and publishing firms, and examines the extent to which new circuits of cultural and literary power emerged. Based on new archival evidence relating to the Transcription Centre, *The Classic* and *The New African*, it includes case studies of Wole Soyinka, Nat Nakasa and Bessie Head, which assess how the authors' careers were affected by these transnational networks and also reveal how they challenged, subverted, and resisted external influence and control.

KEYWORDS: CIA, African literature, cultural cold war, Congress for Cultural Freedom, literary publishing, authorship, Wole Soyinka, Nat Nakasa, Bessie Head

ISBNs: 9781108725545 (PB), 9781108663229 (OC)

ISSNs: 2514-8524 (online), 2514-8516 (print)

Contents

Introduction

In 1961, the US Central Intelligence Agency (CIA) Chief of Covert Action Staff issued a document setting out its covert strategy for international anti-communist propaganda. It announced that books and publishers were to play a fundamental role in the operation: 'Books differ from all other propaganda media primarily because one single book can significantly change the reader's attitude and action to an extent unmatched by the impact of any other single medium'.[1] The document listed the CIA's five-point plan:

(a) Get books published or distributed abroad without revealing any U.S. influence, by covertly subsidizing foreign publications or booksellers.

(b) Get books published which should not be 'contaminated' by any overt tie-in with the U.S. government, especially if the position of the author is 'delicate'.

(c) Get books published for operational reasons, regardless of commercial viability.

(d) Initiate and subsidize indigenous national or international organizations for book publishing or distributing purposes.

(e) Stimulate the writing of politically significant books by unknown foreign authors – either by directly subsidizing the author, if covert contact is feasible, or indirectly, through literary agents or publishers.[2]

This book assesses the implications of the CIA's policy to 'get books published or distributed without revealing any U.S. influence', to directly or indirectly 'subsidiz[e] the author', and to subsidise 'national or international organizations for book publishing'. Focusing on the CIA's cultural programme in Africa, it aims to unravel some of the hidden networks and associations underpinning African literary publishing in this period of decolonisation during the 1960s.

---

[1] Church, *Final Report of the Select Committee*, p. 193. [2] Ibid.

The CIA used two main front organisations to carry out its undercover operation. The flagship of its cultural diplomacy programme was the Congress of Cultural Freedom (CCF), which was established in 1950, with headquarters in Paris and offices in thirty-five countries. It funded art exhibitions, conferences, literary and music prizes, and over twenty prestigious magazines worldwide, including *Encounter* in London; *The Kenyon Review*, *Partisan Review*, and *The New Leader* in the United States; *Der Monat* in Germany; *Preuves* in France; *Quadrant* in Australia; *Tempo Presente* in Italy; *Forum* in Austria; *Jiyu* in Japan; *Cuadernos; Mundo Nuevo* in Latin America; and *Hiwār* in Beirut. The second major front organisation was the Farfield Foundation – an ostensibly philanthropic organisation based in New York, which was incorporated in 1952 as a non-profit organisation, allegedly to 'strengthen the cultural ties which bind the nations of the world and to reveal to all peoples who share the traditions of a free culture the inherent dangers which totalitarianism poses to intellectual and cultural development'.[3] Both the CCF and Farfield also received a limited amount of funding from private philanthropists.[4] The CIA's Africa programme stretched across the continent, with hubs in Cape Town, Johannesburg, Nairobi, Kampala, Ibadan, as well as in Paris and London. It was predominantly a publishing programme, funding a number of literary and political magazines, including *Black Orpheus*, *Transition*, *The New African*, *Africa South*, and *The Classic*, and book publishing by Présence Africaine in Paris, Mbari in Nigeria, and Chemchemi in Kenya. It also funded arts centres, literary festivals and prizes, theatre productions, radio and television broadcasting operations, and conferences.

The technique of enlisting writers and publishers in the production and dissemination of government propaganda creation has a well-established historical precedent in British intelligence services. During the First World War, Charles Masterman used publishers, including Hodder and Stoughton, John Murray, Thomas Nelson, Methuen, and Oxford University Press, as well as a number of authors, including Arthur Conan Doyle, Arnold Bennett, Thomas Hardy, G. K. Chesterton, and H. G. Wells, to produce covert propaganda for the British War Propaganda

---

[3] Saunders, *Cultural Cold War*, p. 126.   [4] Benson, *Black Orpheus*, p. 36.

Bureau at Wellington House in London.[5] During the Second World War, authors including Graham Greene, George Orwell, and John Betjeman, and publishers like Hodder and Stoughton, Oxford University Press, Penguin, Heinemann, Faber, Collins, and Hogarth Press were likewise enlisted into the propaganda machine through the Ministry of Information.[6] In the post-war period, the British government co-opted British publishers to publish colonial propaganda via the auspices of the Colonial Literature Bureaux across Africa.[7] The difference in the case of the CIA was the sheer scale of the operation – its global geographical reach – and its covert nature. Whereas the British government overtly enlisted authors and publishers into its propaganda campaigns and only the readers were deceived about the source of the books, with the CIA, the deception extended to the whole literary establishment – authors, publishers, editors, and readers – none of whom were made aware of the propaganda operation.

The CIA's Cold War publishing strategy was more subtle than simple indoctrination. The CIA chose to influence the 'restricted field of production': the realm of 'high art' and serious literature, poetry, and plays produced by elite, highly educated writers, which Bourdieu describes as claiming to be autonomous and independent of commercial and political influence.[8] The main currency in operation in this field is cultural and symbolic capital; its association with economic and political capital is carefully disguised: it is 'an independent social universe with its own laws of functioning, its specific relations of force, its dominants and its dominated, and so forth'.[9] In order for the CIA to exert influence in the literary sphere, it had to build up credibility within the sphere by infiltrating existing literary

---

[5] Buitenhuis, *Great War of Words*, p. 133.

[6] Holman, *Carefully Concealed Connections*

[7] Davis, 'Creating a Book Empire', p. 136.

[8] Bourdieu, *Field of Cultural Production*, p. 163. I discuss how Bourdieu's theories of cultural production translate to African literary publishing contexts in 'Playing the Game?' and *Creating Postcolonial Literature*. For further analyses of this, see Brouillette, 'Postcolonial Authorship Revisited'; Zimbler, 'For Neither Love nor Money'; and Krishnan, *Contingent Canons*.

[9] Bourdieu, *Field of Cultural Production*, p. 163.

and journalistic groups through financial patronage. Thus, the credibility and symbolic capital of writers and publications depended on the secrecy of the operation, on avoiding any 'overt tie-in with the U.S. government'.

There are two key lines of interpretation of this covert operation. Some regard it as a form of American cultural and political imperialism, while others see it as a benign, essentially apolitical form of cultural patronage and diplomacy. Frances Stoner Saunders's seminal study of the cultural cold war cast the Congress for Cultural Freedom as 'an extensive, highly influential network of intelligence personnel, political strategists, the corporate establishment and old school ties of the Ivy League universities', who successfully infiltrated left-leaning and liberal academic, literary, and cultural associations around the world.[10] Using the metaphor of the patron and the piper to describe the relationship between the CIA and its network of authors and editors across the globe,[11] she disputes claims that the CIA and its foundations provided aid with 'no strings attached' or that the recipients of this funding were unaware of its source.[12]

While Saunders focuses on American and British art and literature in the cultural cold war, Andrew N. Rubin, Juliana Spahr, and Bhakti Shringarpure pursue a similar line of argument with respect to the CIA's impact on world literature and postcolonial literature. Rubin states that the CIA played a defining role in the establishment of 'new regimes of consecration', 'a new kind of international literary system', and a 'whole ideology and mode of world literature', and thereby helped to create world literature along conservative modernist lines by promoting art for art's sake.[13] He argues that the CCF 'upheld an illusion of the literary world outside of politics' and that it gave 'tremendous visibility' to some writers while excluding others.[14] This was part of the 'cultural process by which imperial authority was transferred from Britain and France to the United States in the aftermath of the Second World War'; its aim was to suppress dissent in the face of African nationalism.[15] Bhakti Shringarpure argues that CIA influence was exercised not so much through overt propaganda and

[10] Saunders, *Cultural Cold War*, pp. 1–2. [11] Saunders, *Who Paid the Piper?*

[12] Saunders, *Cultural Cold War*, pp. 4, 377. [13] Rubin, *Archives of Authority*, p. 9.

[14] Ibid., pp. 15–16. [15] Rubin, *Archives of Authority*, pp. 17, 20.

editorial interventions as through promotion, cross-publication, and the creation of a depoliticised postcolonial canon of literature.[16] Juliana Spahr likewise claims that 'it is obvious that these manipulations curbed autonomy', but that the CCF had no need to 'censor or regulate' the publications that they funded, as the editors and writers who received support were 'handpicked by the Congress because their views were sympathetic to its concerns'.[17] These scholars make the astute observation that the CIA influenced postcolonial literature not simply through textual interventions but also by managing a select group of authors' visibility through patronage and promotion, international publication and translation possibilities, literary festivals and prizes. While these are intriguing arguments, all three studies relate to postcolonial literature in general, and further research on African literature is necessary to substantiate these bold claims.

Anecdotal evidence and scholarship related more specifically to the cultural cold war in Africa draws very different conclusions. Writers and editors who were involved in this programme have been at pains to assert their political and literary independence from the CIA after the funding scandal first came to light in 1966–7.[18] Esk'ia Mphahlele, Randolph Vigne, James Currey, Ronald Segal, Rajat Neogy, and Wole Soyinka have all stated that they were unaware of the source of the funding, that it had been provided on an unconditional basis, and that they had absolute freedom to exercise their own editorial judgements. Several subsequent studies of the CCF's little magazines in Africa, specifically *Black Orpheus*,[19] *Transition*,[20] and *Africa South*,[21] have corroborated these views and have found no evidence of editorial interference on the part of the CIA, or knowledge of the CIA funding by editors and authors. The CIA funding of Mbari Publishing offered writers and editors liberation from reliance on market

---

[16] Shringarpure, *Cold War Assemblages*, p. 157.

[17] Spahr, *Du Bois's Telegram*, pp. 105, 102.

[18] Bourdieu, *Field of Cultural Production*, p. 40

[19] Benson, *Black Orpheus*, pp. 115, 36–7.

[20] Rogers, 'Culture in Transition', p. 190, and Kalliney, *Modernism in a Global Context*, pp. 102.

[21] Sandwith, 'Entering the Territory', p. 135, n. 7.

forces or the restrictions of national governments, according to Nathan Suhr-Sytsma.[22] The Africa programme of the CCF is described by Asha Rogers as offering 'non-interventionist sponsorship', with an overriding aim to 'protect cultural autonomy and 'construct robust literary and cultural spheres'.[23] And the Transcription Centre and *Transition* magazine are termed by Peter Kalliney, 'relatively autonomous literary institutions'[24] which supported African writers who were 'drawn to modernist principles of intellectual freedom and writerly detachment'.[25] He claims that 'modernist aesthetic beliefs were key to US cultural diplomacy programs during the early Cold War', that the CCF used the doctrine of aesthetic autonomy 'to recruit intellectuals with no affinity for either Cold War superpower'.[26] These literary historians concur that the CIA's cultural interventions in Africa had limited political impact, and that their main legacy was the support of a transnational literary community with a shared literary aesthetic of modernist autonomy.

This book aims to contribute to these ongoing debates by following two new lines of enquiry. On a macro level, it examines the transnational networks of African literary publishing in the period of decolonisation to investigate whether the CIA was successful in infiltrating African literary institutions, and to determine the extent to which new circuits of cultural and literary power emerged. By concentrating on publishers, the frequently forgotten agents in literary production, I review how publishing alliances were re-formed and realigned during the 1960s. On a micro level, this book focuses on detailed author case studies, which examine whether or how individual African writers' careers and works were shaped by the literary networks supported by the CIA, and how they responded to these interventions. The three writers in question had widely divergent experiences of the CIA-funded institutions. Wole Soyinka was one of the principal beneficiaries of this funding, and the first case study analyses the role of the CIA in contributing to his canonical status. It focuses particularly on the role of

22　Suhr-Sytsma, *Poetry, Print and the Making of Postcolonial Literature*, p. 72.

23　Asha Rogers, 'Officially Autonomous', p. 91.

24　Kalliney, *Modernism in a Global Context*, pp. 153.

25　Kalliney, 'Modernism, African Literature, and the Cold War', p. 333.

26　Ibid., p. 333.

the Transcription Centre in London in supporting Soyinka's writing career, and in facilitating the performance of his plays and the publishing and anthologising of his work. In contrast, the second case study examines the fraught and ultimately tragic involvement of Nat Nakasa with the CIA, charting his difficulties in creating a multiracial, transnational network of African writers as editor of *The Classic*, a literary magazine in Johannesburg that was funded by the Farfield Foundation. The third case study of Bessie Head examines the routes to international publishing open to a writer who was an outsider, on the periphery of the CIA-funded literary network. After reviewing her early involvement with the CCF-funded magazine *The New African*, it then turns to her negotiations with commercial New York and London literary editors and publishers during the publication of her first two novels. This research is based largely on previously overlooked records in the Transcription Centre Records in Austin, Texas; the Nat Nakasa Papers at Wits University, Johannesburg; and the Bessie Head's Papers collection at Serowe, Botswana. The correspondence reveals how these authors' careers were transformed by these transnational networks, as well as the ways in which these writers challenged, subverted, and resisted external influence and control.

The writers within the networks of the CCF constituted a select group who received unprecedented opportunities for international publication and promotion. Authors within these networks, who were direct recipients of CIA patronage, included Soyinka, Chinua Achebe, Esk'ia Mphahlele, Lewis Nkosi, John Pepper Clark-Bekederemo, Christopher Okigbo, Dennis Brutus, Alex La Guma, Grace Okot, Kofi Awooner, and Ama Ata Aidoo, and, to a lesser extent, Ngugi and Head. According to Bernth Lindfors, these writers went on to receive 'the lion's share of attention in African university literature courses' and to become the most cited writers in African literary criticism,[27] gaining top positions in the 'canon of anglophone African writing'.[28] Social networks are described by Bourdieu as a means of transmission and exchange of social capital. He maintains that a 'network of relationships is the product of investment strategies, individual or collective, consciously or unconsciously aimed at establishing or reproducing social relationships that are directly usable in the short or long

---

[27] See Lindfors, 'African Literary Criticism', pp. 6 and 7. [28] Ibid., p. 10.

term',[29] and that these networks operate by principles of exclusion: 'the conservation and accumulation of the capital which is the basis of the group' depends on members of the group regulating 'the conditions of access to the right to declare oneself a member of the group'.[30] A key element of this investigation is, then, understanding not only the 'investment strategies' employed by the CIA but also the 'conditions of access' and exclusion that regulated these networks.

Recent scholarship in African print culture has excavated hidden literature that had been excluded from the canon. Karin Barber designates this the 'obverse' or 'underside' of African literature: the 'profusion of innovative individual writing and enterprising efforts in local, small-scale print publication'.[31] Such vibrant but subsequently neglected literary publishing associations in the period of decolonisation include Hausa literary networks,[32] Swahili post-independence poetry circles,[33] and popular literature magazines in socialist Tanzania.[34] Yet, other critics have drawn attention to the difficulty of literary survival for authors who were cut off from either state patronage or international publication. Joyce Ashuntantang's research on Anglophone Cameroonian literature shows that authors from the region were largely excluded from publication by multinational companies in the post-independence period, for a number of linguistic, political and geographic reasons, and she relates the problems facing dynamic but 'shoe string' literary publishers in Cameroon. Her verdict is that although 'multinational corporations exposed African writers to an international audience, they inadvertently stifled creativity and limited the creative arena'.[35] In a similar vein, Moradewun Adejunmobi argues that Indian Ocean literature is largely invisible to 'institutional readers', having been side-lined by multinational publishing houses, omitted from anthologies of African literature, and subject to critical neglect. Her conclusion is that, 'It will no doubt take the combined efforts of committed writers, editors, and

---

[29] Bourdieu, 'The Forms of Capital', p. 249.

[30] Bourdieu, 'The Forms of Capital', p. 251. [31] Barber, 'Introduction', p. 3.

[32] Furniss, 'Literary Circles'. [33] Askew, 'Everyday Poetry from Tanzania'.

[34] Reuster-Jahn, 'Private Entertainment Magazines'.

[35] Ashuntantang, 'Creative Writing in Cameroon', p. 245.

critics to transform Indian Ocean literature into a more visible and clearly defined entity' within which they 'would constitute dominant rather than marginal voices'.[36] Exclusion from these influential publishing networks has evidently rendered whole sectors of African literature invisible.

This book aims, then, to contribute to an understanding of the 'politics of visibility' of African literature[37] by addressing the CIA's role in the consecration and canonisation of African literature in the 1960s. Very little research has been carried out to date on the economics of the CIA's literary operation in Africa, or on the alliances that were cultivated between the Congress of Cultural Freedom and British and American publishers. Focusing on three individual authors' negotiations with their patrons and publishers, this study sheds new light on the intersecting networks of power and money that shaped African literature in the period of decolonisation, during a period that Soyinka termed a 'second scramble for Africa': a fight for cultural control in which authors, their publishers and the CIA were particularly entangled.[38]

---

[36] Adejunmobi, 'Claiming the Field', p. 1258.

[37] Shringarpure, *Cold War Assemblages*, p. 165.

[38] Soyinka's unpublished preface to *Poems of South Africa*, quoted in Ibironke, *Remapping African Literature*, p. 54.

1 African Literary Publishing during Decolonisation

Several writers and publishers remarked on the dramatic increase in the publication of African literature in the late 1950s and early 1960s. Nat Nakasa, editor of *The Classic*, referred to 'a vigorous, almost frantic, search for African writing';[39] the Ghanaian writer Ellis Ayetey Komey commented that the demand for African literature was outstripping supply;[40] and Diana Athill, editor at André Deutsch, observed that, 'for a time during the fifties and early sixties it was probably easier for a black writer to get his book accepted by a London publisher, and kindly reviewed thereafter, than it was for a young white person'.[41] Literary traffic also began to flow in multiple directions: whereas under British colonial rule, English literature was largely shipped from the metropolitan centre to the colonial peripheries and very few African writers' work was published, in the late 1950s and 1960s new opportunities for publication opened up worldwide. As colonial arrangements for publishing began to break down, a vacuum was left which a number of agencies – state and commercial – were keen to occupy, and new alliances were formed. This chapter examines how these transnational networks of African literary publishing operated and intersected in the period of decolonisation.

Before 1957, African literary publishing in English tended to be carried out from London. Initially, this was by London-based religious publishers; for example, the Religious Tract Society published Samuel Ntara's *Man of Africa* (1934), the Society for the Promotion of Christian Knowledge published Thomas Mofolo's *The Traveller to the East* (1934), and Joseph Kwame Danquah's *The Third Woman* (1943) was published by the United Society for Christian Literature. By the mid 1940s, a few small commercial firms in London had published a select number of African writers: Peter Abrahams (Dorothy Crisp and Faber), Amos Tutuola (Faber), Camara Laye (Collins), and Cyprian Ekwensi (Nelson). Lutterworth published a selection of West African short stories, and Stockwell, a small imprint in Ilfracombe, Devon, published Ghanaian poetry and novels in the 1940s and

---

[39] Nakasa, 'Comment', *The Classic*, 1:2, 5.

[40] Komey, 'Wanted: Creative Writers', 63. [41] Athill, *Stet*, p. 103.

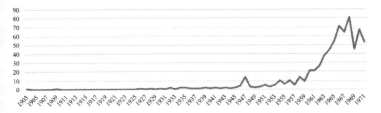

Figure 1 Number of African literary titles in English published worldwide, 1903–72

1950s. Some of these writers, including Abrahams, Laye, and Tutuola, were co-published by the New York publishers Knopf, Grove Press, the Noonday Press, and John Day. Only a handful of works were published in Africa. In South Africa, these included Sol Plaatje's *Mhudi* (Lovedale, 1930), Herbert Isaac Earnest Dhlomo's *The Girl Who Killed to Save* (Lovedale, 1935), and Ezekiel Mphahlele's *Man Must Live and Other Stories* (African Bookman, 1947); in Accra, the popular novellas of Gilbert A. Sam and J. Beninbengor Blay were published by Gilisam Publishing Syndicate, while Cyprian Ekwensi's short stories were published by Chuks Services in Yaba, Lagos. During the colonial period, African literary publishing in the English language was thus both limited and predominantly London centred.

In the period of decolonisation, there was a striking increase in the number of African literary titles published in the English language, as illustrated in Figure 1.[42] Of the total number of works of African literature published in the period 1900–72, 87 per cent were published after 1957, the year of Ghanaian independence.

This rapid growth in literary publishing was mainly linked to the expansion of British educational publishing in Africa. There was a period of investment in education on the part of the newly independent African governments, and British publishers capitalised on this by setting up branches and subsidiary

---

[42] I have carried out this quantitative analysis of African literary production between 1900 and 1972, based on bibliographical data gathered by Donald Herdeck in *African Authors*.

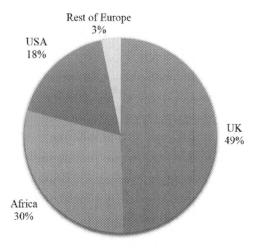

Figure 2 Place of publication of African literary titles in English, 1957–72

companies across the continent. Oxford University Press (OUP) and Longmans converted their sales offices in Nigeria and Kenya to publishing branches or subsidiary companies, and Nelson established publishing branches in Ikeja (near Lagos) and in Nairobi. The British book trade in Africa was strongly supported by the British government, via the British Council and the Arts Council, while international copyright legislation and the post-war publishing trade agreements carved up English-speaking world markets between American and British publishers and helped ensure the maintenance of British publishers' dominance in the former British colonies.[43] This meant that publishers based in Africa were able to obtain rights to distribute a book only nationally rather than internationally; they had to obtain co-publishing arrangements with British or American publishers for their books to be sold internationally, with the result that African authors who sought an international market for their books were compelled to seek a British or American publisher.

These factors led to the persistence of the colonial model of African literary publishing (see Figure 2). Of the 692 African literary titles published

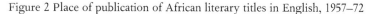

[43] Hench, *Books as Weapons*, p. 198.

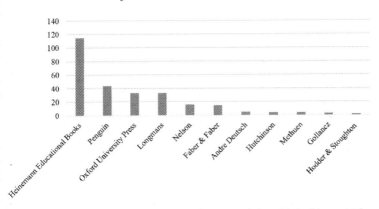

Figure 3 Number of African literary titles in English published by British publishers, 1957–72

in the English language in the period 1957–72, 49 per cent were published in the United Kingdom, 30 per cent in Africa, 18 per cent in the United States, and the remaining 3 per cent in other European countries.

Heinemann Educational Books, by far the most significant of the British publishing firms involved in African literature, published 115 titles in the African Writers Series from 1962 to 1972. In the same period, Penguin published forty-four titles, Longmans and Oxford University Press each published thirty-three, and Nelson published sixteen. By contrast, the output of the more prestigious London literary publishers was more limited. Faber and Faber issued fifteen titles, but Andre Deutsch, Hutchinson, Methuen, Gollancz, and Hodder & Stoughton published only a handful of works of African literature (see Figure 3).

There was also a marked increase in the number of works in English published by African publishers from 1957 to 1972, although they struggled to compete in the face of British and American publishers' dominance in this market. During this period, 30 per cent of new African literary titles were

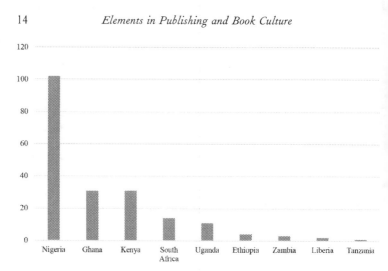

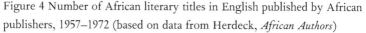

Figure 4 Number of African literary titles in English published by African publishers, 1957–1972 (based on data from Herdeck, *African Authors*)

published in Africa, but the profile across the continent was very uneven. According to Herdeck's bibliography, a total of 102 new literary titles were issued in Nigeria, 31 titles in Ghana and Kenya, 14 in South Africa, 11 in Uganda, and a negligible number in Ethiopia, Zambia, Liberia, and Tanzania (Figure 4).

During the period of decolonisation, American publishers also mounted a challenge to the British monopoly over this market but, as Figure 5 shows, this was limited to a very small number of publishing companies. Collier-Macmillan was the leading American publisher of African literature, issuing twelve titles including works by Camara Laye, Wole Soyinka, Peter Abrahams, and Ngũgĩ wa Thiong'o; Doubleday published the work of Legson Kariya, Ama Ata Aidoo, Ayi Kwei Armah, and Kofi Awooner; Hill & Wang published the plays of Wole Soyinka, Lewis Nkosi, James Henshaw, and Henry Ofori; Crowell published the poetry of Cosmo Pieterse and James Rubadiri, and a play by Joseph Okpaku; while Simon & Schuster published a novel by Bessie Head. The majority of these American publishers

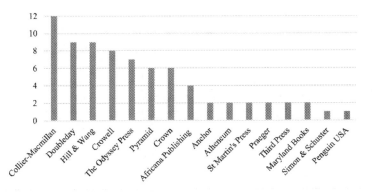

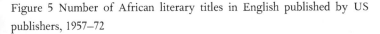

Figure 5 Number of African literary titles in English published by US publishers, 1957–72

were involved in the publication of co-editions with London publishers, or reprints of works that had already been published in Europe, and their attention was focused on a few star African authors.

This brief overview of the publishing environment for African literature demonstrates that there was a significant increase in African literary publishing after decolonisation. African and American firms increasingly competed for a share in this growing market, but British publishing firms continued to be the dominant players. I turn now to assess the impact of CIA interventions on this persistent colonial model of African literary production.

'A Missionary Move'

In 1980, Jack Thompson, executive director of the Farfield Foundation, was questioned by Peter Benson about the reasons for the CIA's covert operation in African literature. Thompson's response was revealing:

> Our particular interest was in literary people ... We thought it would be important to aid them because it seemed to us, on the basis of the political experience of other

countries, that literary intellectuals had been important. Our interest was in establishing an independent publishing program . . . In those innocent days, incredible as it may seem, my theory was that if they were intelligent they were good . . . I think now, looking back on it, that it was probably in the long run, indirectly and obscurely, part of American imperialism. Americans tended to take over these markets from England, but I certainly didn't know that then. As I look back on it, it was basically a missionary move. I would oppose it now. But it seemed like a good idea at the time . . . There were no strings attached whatever.[44]

Thompson posits two key reasons for the CIA operation. First, its main concern was political volatility in Africa and the need for a stabilising intellectual elite; he frames it as an attempt to create a community of 'literary intellectuals' by offering them funding with 'no strings attached'. Secondly, he claims that this was an act of 'American imperialism', particularly in terms of its support of an 'independent publishing program' and its foray into British book markets. Thompson's arguments raise important questions about the underlying rationale for the CIA's investment in African literature and culture, and the extent to which it affected African literary production.

The CIA's covert involvement in African literature was orchestrated jointly by the Congress of Cultural Freedom in Paris and the Farfield Foundation in New York. Its initial 'missionary move', in the words of Thompson, involved a series of tours of Africa; for example, Thompson himself visited South Africa where he met Lewis Nkosi and Nat Nakasa in 1960.[45] This was followed by a series of cross-continental workshops, conferences, prizes, and events for African writers and publishers, by which the CIA actively cultivated connections with the literary elite and intelligentsia. Potential leaders were identified and offered funding to support their existing literary magazines or to establish new ones. In certain cases, they were also offered funding to establish hubs for African literature in English across the continent. A number of African writers were provided

---

[44] Thompson, in Benson, *Black Orpheus*, p. 36. [45] Benson, *Black Orpheus*, p. 35.

with opportunities for publication in the magazines funded by the CCF, as well as by CCF-funded book publishers, and close associations were formed with commercial publishers in the United Kingdom and the United States for anthologising and republishing these works. The result was an interwoven system of literary patronage and support, and the creation of a system of literary hubs that were financially dependent on the CIA.

The first of these hubs was in Ibadan, Nigeria. This was set up by Ulli Beier, a German extra-mural lecturer based at Ibadan University, after he attended the first Africa-related event of the CCF, the 1956 World Congress of African Writers and Artists in Paris, organised by Mercer Cook, the CCF's first Director of African Services. Inspired by the event, Beier decided on his return to Ibadan to launch the magazine *Black Orpheus*, which he did in 1957, with the objective of supporting and publishing African writers from all parts of Africa, as well as from North and South America. The magazine was at first edited by Beier, together with Wole Soyinka and Ezekiel Mphahlele, and initially it was supported by the General Publications Section of the Ministry of Education, Ibadan; a government organisation set up to promote western Nigerian literature. When the funding ran out in 1960, Mphahlele applied to John Thompson of the Farfield Foundation for further funding, which was granted. Beier was then invited to Paris to meet Michael Josselson, international director of Farfield, and was offered further financial support for the establishment of the Ibadan-based Mbari Writers and Artists Club, an arts centre with a theatre, gallery, library, and publishing imprint.[46] This was established in 1961 as a meeting place for young poets, writers, and intellectuals like Chinua Achebe, Wole Soyinka, J. P. Clark, and Christopher Okigbo, with Mphahlele as its founder and first president. Mbari became the blueprint for the CCF's plan for seemingly decolonised African literature, and the plan was to expand this model across the continent.

Mphahlele took over the role of director of the African Services of the CCF after Cook's resignation in 1961. Based in Paris and working with John Hunt, executive director of the CCF, he led the expansion of the CCF's Africa programme into South and East Africa, beginning with a 'tour throughout Africa ... to look for writers and artists who need to be

[46] Coleman, *Liberal Conspiracy*, pp. 203–4.

sponsored and should be acquainted with Mbari'.[47] A major milestone was the Conference of African Writers of English Expression organised by Mphahlele at Makerere College in Kampala, Uganda, in June 1962. This brought together forty-five delegates to discuss the future of African literature in English, including African authors, academics, publishers, and broadcasters. Invited delegates included James Ngũgĩ (later Ngũgĩ wa Thiong'o), Chinua Achebe, Wole Soyinka, Alex La Guma, Bloke Modisane, and American guests of honour Langston Hughes and Ralph Ellison. A number of publishers attended, including editors of African literary magazines Neville Rubin (*The New African*) and Rajat Neogy (*Transition*), book publishers including Andre Deutsch and Van Milne from Thomas Nelson, as well as Roger Norrington from Oxford University Press, and a representative from Longmans. Only three of the invited participants were women: Rebecca Njau, Grace Ogot, and Efua Sutherland.[48] The conference was an important step in establishing a public forum for the debate and discussion of African literature in English.[49] None of the participants were aware of the CIA's funding of the conference; indeed, Ngũgĩ wrote, 'This secret manipulation was typical of the Cold War environment in which the conference and the decolonisation of Africa took place ... For me and the other participants it was simply a gathering of writers'.[50] Elsewhere, he wrote that the CIA funding of Makerere was evidence that 'certain directions in our cultural political, and economic choices can be masterminded from the metropolitan centres of imperialism'.[51]

Mphahlele's attempts to build up the work of the CCF in East Africa proved to be more of a struggle. In 1962 he set up the Chemchemi Cultural Centre in Nairobi, on the same model as Mbari, with the aim to encourage new writers in Kenya.[52] However, it was slow to develop. After visiting

---

[47] Mphahlele, 'Mbari: First Anniversary', p. 7.   [48] 1.3, TC/HRC.

[49] An earlier conference funded by the CIA, which aimed to strengthen universities in West Africa, was the Inter-University Cooperation in West Africa (Freetown) in December 1961.

[50] Ngũgĩ wa Thiong'o, *Birth of a Dream Weaver*, p. 139.

[51] Ngũgĩ wa Thiong'o, *Decolonising the Mind*, p. 30 n. 2.

[52] Coleman, *Liberal Conspiracy*, p. 205.

Chemchemi in February 1965, Dennis Duerden of the Transcription Centre in London recounted its various shortcomings to John Thompson: there were, in his view, too many rival cultural and arts centres in Nairobi, and he worried that there was little creative inspiration in Kenya compared to Nigeria and Ghana. He also considered Mphahlele to be bureaucratic in his approach, and thought his big house and large salary aroused local suspicion.[53] Eventually, the CCF decided to stop funding the centre, and Mphahlele had to concede defeat.[54] It was evidently regarded as overfunded and inauthentic: an illusion of independence and autonomy was evidently vital to the success of these CIA initiatives.

The model of literary and cultural investment established by the CCF appeared to reverse the colonial flows of literary traffic from the metropole to Africa. New literary hubs were created across Africa that promoted local management and local literary production, and, where successful, they gave an illusion of the creation of a decentralised, avant-garde small-press culture, but, as the experience of Chemchemi shows, the reliance of these hubs on American money and influence had to be carefully concealed.

'*A New Publishing Program*'

After Makerere, the CIA funded a number of literary magazines across the continent. At the conference, Mphahlele invited several of the existing magazine editors to apply for sponsorship. Rajat Neogy, a Ugandan-born Bengali, had launched his cultural and literary magazine *Transition* in November 1961 from Kampala, shortly before Ugandan independence, but after four issues he ran out of money. He applied to the CCF and received funding for the following six years, although he complained constantly about the 'shoe string' finances of the CCF.[55] *Transition* became one of the foremost literary-political magazines in Africa, with the largest circulation of all the CCF magazines in Africa, reaching 12,000 worldwide, including 3,000 in the United States.[56] Other literary magazines that received funding from the CCF were *The New*

---

[53] Letter, Duerden to Thompson, 9 February 1965, 23.4, TC/HRC.

[54] Manganyi, *Exiles and Homecomings*, p. 236.

[55] Letter, Neogy to Duerden, 20 June 1963, 17.17, TC/HRC.

[56] Coleman, *Liberal Conspiracy*, p. 191.

African, *Africa South*, *Contrast*, and the *West Africa Review*. The financial support offered by the CCF to these magazines appears to have been quite uneven. In 1966, *The New African* in London received $15,000, *Black Orpheus* in Ibadan received only $2,500, and, despite Neogy's complaints, *Transition* in Kampala received the largest grant of $25,000.[57]

In addition to these so-called 'little magazines', the CCF funded a number of small literary presses for the publication of book-length works of African literature. The largest of these was Mbari Publishing, in Ibadan. The first titles were by francophone African writers, but gradually Nigerian writers and South African writers were published, including John Pepper Clark's *Song of a Goat* (1961) and *Poems* (1962), Alex La Guma's *A Walk in the Night* (1962), Christopher Okigbo's poetry collection *Heavensgate* (1962), Dennis Brutus's collection of poetry, *Sirens, Knuckles, Boots* (1963), and Lenrie Peters's *Poems* (1964). The imprint had the appearance of a grass-roots, independent operation, and many literary historians continue to regard it in this light. Martin Klammer, for example, claims that it was established 'in order to develop a pan-African literature, culture and art based in Africa and independent of London- or Paris-based publishers'.[58] Chemchemi Cultural Centre, meanwhile, published only one work: a short poetic tribute to Jomo Kenyatta by Joseph Kariuki, entitled *Ode to Mzee* (1964). The other book publishing enterprises supported by the CCF were Seven Seas in Berlin, which published a new edition of Ezekiel Mphahlele's autobiography *Down Second Avenue* (1962), Richard Rive's short story collection *African Songs* (1963), and Alex La Guma's two novels *And a Threefold Cord* (1964) and *The Stone Country* (1967). The Paris-based magazine *Présence Africaine* also published occasional book-length African literature in English and French, including Efua Sutherland's play *Anansegora* (1964) and a collection of poetry, *New Sum of Poetry*, published in 1964, which included the work of Ama Ata Aidoo, Kofi Awooner, Dennis Brutus, Michael Echeruo, Tsege Gabre-Medhin, and Raymond Kunene.

The political objectives underlying this African literary programme of the CIA continue to confound scholars, because of the contradictions in its

[57] Ibid., p. 276. [58] La Guma with Klammer, *In the Dark*, p. 110.

publication strategy, in particular its publication of the work of writers who were closely involved in the Communist Party. For example, Dennis Brutus had close associations with the South African Communist Party, while Alex La Guma was a party member, and both writers were banned in South Africa under the Suppression of Communism Act.[59] Likewise, questions remain over the CIA's sponsorship of *Africa South*, which published the work of 'Communist Party stalwarts, Unity Movement activists, trade union leaders, ANC cadres', amongst others.[60] Corinne Sandwith concludes that the CIA by these means 'unwittingly endorsed, and helped to spread, the views of well-known South African Communists'.[61] Mphahlele's explanation for this ideological inconsistency was that individuals associated with the CIA programme as organisers and editors, like himself, were given a free hand to select their own authors and books, and he concluded that the CIA 'does not know some of the activities it sponsors'.[62] In his view, the covert nature of the operation led to the political message being diffused and contradictory.

According to Jack Thompson, the CIA's main purpose in funding African literary publishing was not so much to produce political propaganda as to exert American imperialism in a broader sense. In particular, he considered it part of a US challenge to traditional British book markets. However, the close cooperation between the CCF and British commercial publishers casts doubt on this interpretation. The most important of these partnerships was that between Longmans and Mbari in the publication of *Black Orpheus*. When the Ministry of Education in Nigeria was unable to continue funding the magazine in 1963, the *Black Orpheus* editors entered negotiations with Longmans for the production and distribution of the magazine, and Julian Rea agreed to co-publish the magazine in partnership with Mbari for a trial period from 1964 to 1967. In a letter to the directors of Longmans, Julian Rea explained the decision to take on the magazine as a means of enhancing the firm's reputation as a literary publisher in Africa: 'The publication of this magazine is particularly important in terms of our overall African business as it will give us prestige in the field of African

---

[59] Ibid., p. 168–9. [60] Sandwith, 'Entering the Territory', p. 127.
[61] Ibid., p. 135, n. 7. [62] Mphahlele, 'Mphahlele on the CIA', p. 6.

creative writing in which we have had none before'.[63] The arrangement was that Mbari would retain copyright but Longmans would have first option on the reissue of material in the magazine, and Beier's contract with Longmans stipulated that the 'non-political character of the work will be retained'.[64] The arrangement lasted from December 1964 (volume 16) until 1967 (volume 22). In addition to *Black Orpheus*, Longmans also published an anthology of African and Afro-American short stories drawn from the first fourteen issues of the magazine. Published in 1964 with the same title, *Black Orpheus*, this was edited by Ulli Beier, and included the work of Camara Laye, Wilson Harris, Birago Diop, Ezekiel Mphahlele, and Cyprian Ekwensi. However, in 1966, during the Nigerian Civil War, Beier left Ibadan, Achebe joined the Biafrans, Soyinka was imprisoned, and Christopher Okigbu was tragically killed. The Mbari Club closed and *Black Orpheus* suspended publication.

Instead of competing with established British literary publishers, as John Thompson claimed, the CCF worked closely with them in the development of these writers' works. For many authors, publication in a CIA-funded magazine marked the beginning of an illustrious career as a writer, and their work was thereafter published by London- and New York-based publishers. Prominent authors whose early work was published in CCF magazines include the Nigerian writers Wole Soyinka, John Pepper Clark, Gabriel Okara, Obi Egbuna, and Christopher Okigbo; the Ghanaian writers Ama Ata Aidoo, Efua Sutherland, and Kofi Awooner; the South African writers Dennis Brutus, Bessie Head, Alex La Guma, Richard Rive, Arthur Maimane, James Matthews, and Lewis Nkosi; the Kenyan writers Ngũgĩ wa Thiong'o, Joseph Kariuki, Rebecca Njau, and Grace Ogot; the Cameroonian poet Mbella Sonne Dipoko; the Ethiopian writer Tsegaye Gabre-Medhin; the Ugandan writer Robert Serumaga; and the Gambian poet Lenrie Peters. In all these cases, publication in the CIA-funded magazine was followed by publication by British and American publishers. In London, the main publishers of African literature were Heinemann (African Writers Series), Penguin Books, Oxford University Press,

[63] Letter, CJR [Julian Rea] to Directors, 2 July 1963, p. 3, Box 285, Folder 22, 1393, RUL.

[64] Kalliney, 'Modernism, African Literature and the Cold War', p. 355.

Longmans, Rex Collings, Faber and Faber, and Andre Deutsch. The New York firms were the Africana Publishing Corporation, Hill & Wang, Crowell, Doubleday and John Day, Simon & Schuster, and the Third Press. The CCF and commercial publishers worked together to provide a select group of authors with greater international prominence and visibility.

The CIA's publishing network operated at the local, national, and international levels. While this represented a new form of American influence, the magazines and publishing presses supported by the CCF did not seek to compete directly with British commercial firms; instead, the editors worked closely with British publishers in forming symbiotic relationships in the publishing and promotion of African literature. Despite the appearance of devolution of literary power to the margins, the CIA in fact contributed to the hegemony of London and New York as geographical centres of anglophone literary publishing.

'Literary Intellectuals': The Transcription Centre in London

In addition to establishing literary magazines across Africa, the CIA also set up the Transcription Centre as a strategic hub for African literature and culture in London. This was managed by Duerden, who had originally worked for the BBC Africa Services, with responsibility for the BBC's Hausa programme. The CCF first invited Duerden in 1961 to carry out a month-long trip to West and East Africa to plan a series of programmes on African art and literature,[65] and it was here that he met Chinua Achebe, who worked for the BBC in Nigeria. Duerden was thereafter offered a long-term position by the CCF to set up the Transcription Centre in London, which was funded directly by the Farfield Foundation from 1964.[66] Located in prestigious premises near the Strand, it served as a meeting place for African writers and artists in London.

---

[65] Letter, G. Gaymer to Duerden, 20 June 1961, 23.1, TC/HRC.

[66] Letter, Duerden to Thompson, 29 October 1963, 23.4, TC/HRC. The Transcription Centre received an annual grant of £12,500, in addition to Duerden's salary.

The Transcription Centre made 100 radio programmes each year, largely about African culture and writers, on subjects like 'Portraits of African Writers' and 'African Playwrights'. It had a programme of weekly interviews with writers and other key African figures, and a weekly 'Africa Abroad' programme, which had series on issues such as 'African and Afro-American Literature', and other political and socio-economic matters. By December 1966, the centre had recorded around 1,000 tapes, which were broadcast in Tanzania, Zambia, Uganda, Nigeria, Sierra Leone, and Ghana. Some of these were sold to American universities, for example, to the Africa Studies Centre, University of California. In addition to creating radio programmes, the Transcription Centre helped organise and fund theatre production and films. It became the pre-eminent means of promoting African writers and their publications internationally.

The Transcription Centre provided African writers who arrived in the United Kingdom with various means of support. It employed a number of writers, provided temporary accommodation in a flat in central London that was rented by the centre, and was the main conduit for dispersing grants and travel grants to African writers and musicians from the Farfield Foundation. Lewis Nkosi was employed as a journalist and broadcaster from 1964 to March 1965.[67] The Ugandan playwright Robert Serumaga was employed in 1965 for the production of radio programmes, in particular *African Affairs*, until he returned to Uganda to open a theatre.[68] In 1966, Richard Rive[69] and Christopher Okigbo[70] did some piecemeal work for Duerden, and, in 1968, La Guma,[71] Ama Ata Aidoo,[72] and Kofi Awooner (then known as George Awooner-Williams) all worked for the centre.[73] The centre also administered grants from Farfield to Awooner, Achebe, and Ama Ata Aidoo.[74] After 1966, however, Duerden's budget from Farfield was substantially reduced, and he was

---

[67] 17.18, TC/HRC. [68] 17.30/TC/HRC. [69] 17.25, TC/HRC.

[70] 17.22, TC/HRC. [71] 17.9, TC/HRC.

[72] Letter, Duerden to Platt, 25 March 1968, 23.3, TC/HRC. [73] Ibid.

[74] Letter, Platt to Duerden, 24 September 1968, 16.11, TC/HRC; Letter, Aidoo to Duerden, 20 August 1968, 16.12, TC/HRC.

forced to tell writers, including Richard Rive[75] and Christopher Okigbo,[76] that he was no longer able to support them.

In addition to forming links with African writers, the centre also formed close links with British publishers who were engaged in African literature. The centre's newletter, *Cultural Events in Africa*, edited by Diana Speed, offered advertising space to all the major publishers for their new Africa-related titles.[77] Duerden worked particularly closely with Rex Collings from Oxford University Press, whose London office was next door to the Transcription Centre. In establishing the Three Crowns Series, Collings published many of the authors who were connected to the CCF, especially Wole Soyinka, who went on to be a figurehead for the series (see Chapter 2). Collings also published *The Rhythm of Violence* by Lewis Nkosi,[78] who was employed by the CCF, and the short story collection *The Truly Married Woman and Other Stories* by Abioseh Nicol, who organised the 1961 CCF Inter-University Co-operation in West Africa conference in Freetown. Collings republished several books in the Three Crowns Series that had previously been published by Mbari and Présence Africaine, for example *Prose and Poetry* by Leopold Senghor (OUP, 1965) and John Pepper Clark's *Three Plays* (OUP, 1964). Duerden even drew the illustration on the front cover of Clark's book, which unfortunately Clark disliked.[79]

Duerden was also associated with Ronald Segal, former editor of the CCF-funded *Africa South* (1956–60) and *Africa South in Exile* (1960–1), and editor of the Penguin African Library from 1961 to 1975. He carried out recording work for the Transcription Centre in 1964, for which he was paid £200.[80] However, Jack Thompson was cautious about Duerden getting publicly involved with Segal, because of his anti-apartheid political activism. When Segal approached the Transcription Centre in 1964 to ask if he would be interested in broadcasting the Apartheid Conference, Thompson expressed his reluctance: 'I would like to help them, but obviously it is too directly political for a foundation to get involved in'.[81] He suggested that

[75] 17.25, TC/HRC. [76] 17.22, TC/HRC.
[77] Letter, Speed to Keith Sanbrook, 12 November 1964, 14.7, TC/HRC.
[78] Letter, Duerden to Nkosi, 9 June 1964, 17.18, TC/HRC. [79] 17.1, TC/HRC.
[80] Letter, Duerden to Thompson, 5 May 1964, 23.4, TC/HRC.
[81] Letter, Thompson to Duerden, 23 March 1964, 23.4, TC/HRC.

Duerden offer Segal £200 for the radio rights and advised him to obtain the papers from the conference for *Transition*, or another CCF publication, if Segal did not intend to publish them in Penguin. The other publisher that Duerden worked with closely was Andre Deutsch, who had recently embarked on a new venture in African publishing. After the Makerere conference, Deutsch began joint publishing arrangements with the East African Publishing House and Africa University Press. Deutsch arranged for Dennis Duerden to be paid a retainer for suggesting manuscripts to him for Africa University Press and his main London lists.[82]

The Transcription Centre not only promoted African writers internationally through radio programmes that were broadcast across Africa, but was also a means of coordinating African 'literary intellectuals' with London publishers.

'No Strings Attached'

The revelations about the CIA's covert literary activities in the US press in 1966–7 resulted in a public controversy. The story emerged slowly in the *New York Times*, first in a front-page article of 27 April 1966 linking the CCF, and specifically *Encounter*, to the CIA, and then a year later, after an exposé in *Ramparts*, a further *New York Times* article revealed that the CCF had acknowledged receiving funds from the CIA.[83] These allegations led to Stephen Spender and Frank Kermode resigning from *Encounter* and John Hunt and Michael Josselson resigning from the CCF, although Josselson insisted that 'the Congress for Cultural Freedom has worked in entire independence from the CIA'.[84]

Rajat Neogy expressed his bitterness and sense of betrayal that the 'cultural freedom' propagated by the CCF was an elaborate hoax and that his reputation had been discredited. In an interview published in the *Sunday Nation* in June 1967, he denounced the CIA's actions as a 'corruption of human rights that exploited the integrity of his publication', which had caused him to slip into a 'massive two month depression', and voiced his 'resentment at having one's work of more than five years tarred over by this CIA brush'.[85] He emphasised,

---

[82] 11.3, TC/HRC.   [83] Keany, 'Sophiatown Shebeens', p. 120.

[84] Quoted in Coleman, *Liberal Conspiracy*, p. 232.

[85] Neogy and Hill, 'Liberalism', 312.

however, that '*Transition* is not published for the benefits of the CIA or even the fundamental interests of the USA. It exists as a forum of free discussion', and stressed the integrity and independence of the magazine: 'Neither the Congress, nor anybody else has ever once hinted to us what our policy should be'.[86]

Mphahlele's reaction, published in the December 1967–January 1968 issue of *Transition*, reiterated that the funding had been offered with no strings attached, that it had not been imposed on anyone, and that he himself had been in ignorance about its source:

> Yes, the CIA stinks. ... We were had. But in Africa, we have done nothing with the knowledge that the money came from the CIA; nor have we done anything we would not have done if the money had come from elsewhere. I think in the area, it is being credited with more intelligence than there is evidence of. ... We must naturally bite our lips in indignation when we learn the CIA has been financing our projects. But it is dishonest to pretend that the value of what has been thus achieved is morally tainted.[87]

Mphahlele claimed that he had accepted his position at the CCF on the condition that Africa would not be 'turned into another theatre of the Cold War'. He insisted that the CCF did not impose its financial aid on any organisation, that Africans working with the assistance of the CCF had no knowledge that the money came from the CIA, and that their activities would have been carried out regardless of the source of the funding.[88]

Despite Mphahalele's and Neogy's protestations of political independence, the funding scandal decimated the Africa programme of the CCF. In August 1968, further revelations were published in *Ramparts* about the extent of the CIA support of the African programme, and in particular about the sponsorship of *Transition*.[89] The police raided *Transition*'s offices, arresting and imprisoning Neogy and two contributors, Abu Mayanja and Steve Lion, for sedition, after the magazine criticised President Milton

[86] Ibid., pp. 314, 312. [87] Mphahlele, 'Mphahlele on the CIA', p. 6. [88] Ibid., p. 5. [89] Friendly, 'Slick African Magazine', p. 3.

Obote's proposed constitutional reforms. They were sentenced to six months in prison, and Neogy was labelled a CIA agent. Neogy was eventually released, but this was to mark the end of *Transition* in Uganda.[90]

In 1967, the CCF and the Farfield Foundation were closed down. By this stage, the Chemchemi centre had already closed, after Mphahlele left Nairobi in 1966. *Black Orpheus* was published on a very intermittent and ad hoc basis from 1968 to 1993. Funding for the Transcription Centre was discontinued after 1968, and hopes that it could be self-sufficient proved unfounded. *The New African* closed in 1968, and only *The Classic* continued for a while under the editorship of Barney Simon. But the entire literary operation of the CCF in Africa was undermined by the revelation of CIA backing and the realisation that these ostensibly local and autonomous operations had in fact been funded by the American state.[91]

Conclusion

The CIA contributed to a rapid change in anglophone African literary publishing in the period of decolonisation, as it invested in local circuits of literary production across Africa, from Ibadan, Lagos, Accra, Nairobi, and Kampala to Johannesburg and Cape Town. These assisted in the discovery and support of new writers and the nurture of new talent. Its method was to infiltrate existing literary and cultural associations and publishing houses, in order to take advantage of their prestige and connections. In doing so, it exercised a stake in the African literary field, and gained what Bourdieu would call 'monopoly of literary legitimacy'.[92] Offering 'no strings attached' funding to cash-strapped little magazines across the continent, the CIA gained unique access to these communities of 'literary intellectuals' and close connections were established between the writers and the American patrons. This was the covert means by which the United States exerted its cultural imperialism. However, its modus operandi was not, as Jack Thompson attested, to directly challenge British

---

[90] Coleman, *Liberal Conspiracy*, p. 192.

[91] See Holt, 'Bread or Freedom', pp. 97–102, for an analysis of the implication of these funding revelations for the Beirut-based CCF journal *Hiwãr*.

[92] Bourdieu, *Field of Cultural Production*, p. 42.

publishers' dominance in the continent, but instead to form alliances with established and prestigious British publishers to amplify the influence of the writers and publications it supported across Africa. As a result of these opportunities, a small number of privileged African authors rose rapidly to prominence and global recognition. How these CIA-funded institutions affected the lives and work of individual authors is the subject of the next three chapters.

2 Wole Soyinka, the Transcription Centre, and the CIA

Wole Soyinka has a reputation as the African literary celebrity par excellence. He became the first black African to win the Nobel Prize for Literature in 1986, and has received a string of other cultural honours and achievements, including professorial posts at the University of Ife, Cornell University, Emory University, and the University of Nevada, and scholar-in-residence appointments at Loyola Marymount University and Duke University. By the mid 1980s, Soyinka was the most frequently assigned author on reading lists in universities across anglophone West, East, and Central Africa and his work, along with Achebe's, had received the most attention by literary scholars and critics.[93] He has a prominent role as a poet-intellectual and an international campaigner for human rights, and is currently a celebrity advocate for UNESCO. Listed as the most powerful living African writer by Forbes,[94] Soyinka is at the forefront of African literary celebrity culture, a phenomenon termed by Chidi Amuta a 'culture of messianism'.[95]

There has been much speculation about the extent to which the CIA initiated Soyinka's initial meteoric rise to fame and international recognition. Soyinka himself has denied any awareness at the time of CIA backing of the Congress for Cultural Freedom and the Farfield Foundation, and wrote in his memoir of his reaction when the CIA connections were revealed:

> Soon enough . . . we would discover that we had been dining, and with relish, with the original of that serpentine incarnation the devil, romping in our postcolonial Garden of Eden and gorging on the fruits of the Tree of Knowledge! Nothing – virtually no project, no cultural initiative – was left un-brushed by the CIA's reptilian coils. The first All-African Congress of African Writers and Intellectuals in Makerere, Uganda, after the winds of independence blew across the continent, had been sponsored by the Congress for Cultural Freedom and

[93] Lindfors, 'African Literature Criticism', p. 9–11.

[94] Nsehe, 'The 40 Most Powerful Celebrities in Africa'.

[95] Amuta, *Theory of African Literature*, p. 29.

Encounter. The same source infiltrated *Transition* magazine, the pioneering journal of ideas in postcolonial Africa, under the editorship of an East African Indian of Brahmin extraction, Rajat Neogy. That a certain U.S.-based Farfield foundation, which lavishly expended its resources on the continent's postcolonial intellectual thought and creativity, was a front for the American CIA![96]

The CIA's 'reptilian coils' over Soyinka's own life extended from *Black Orpheus* and Mbari to the Makerere Conference, *Encounter*, *Transition*, and the Transcription Centre in London, but scholarly opinion is divided as to the implications of these connections. Andrew Rubin argues that the CIA's programme of author promotion – its 'self-reflexive, self-aggrandizing, and self-serving activities' – served to manage Soyinka's reputation and visibility,[97] while Juliana Spahr alleges that Soyinka had 'unusually close ties to the US government', even to the point of frequently meeting with US intelligence in the late 1970s.[98] By contrast, Peter Kalliney insists that Soyinka's acceptance of patronage from the CCF does not suggest that he was a puppet of the United States, but that it points to a convergence of interests with the CCF, in terms of their shared concern with 'experimental modernism', autonomy and 'independence from the Cold War's ideological binaries'.[99] These opinions are based, however, on limited research regarding the CIA's precise involvement in Soyinka's career. This chapter draws on under-explored archival records of the Congress for Cultural Freedom and the Transcription Centre to further investigate how Soyinka's early career as a writer was affected by these enmeshed associations with the CIA.

The CCF, the Transcription Centre, and the Promotion of Soyinka, 1960–5

Soyinka's multiple affiliations with the Congress for Cultural Freedom began in Ibadan in the early 1960s. As mentioned previously, he was co-

[96] Soyinka, *You Must Set Forth*, p. 40. [97] Rubin, *Archives of Authority*, p. 65.
[98] Spahr, *Du Bois's Telegram*, p. 94.
[99] Kalliney, 'Modernism, African Literature, and the Cold War', p. 333.

editor of the literary magazine *Black Orpheus* from 1959 to 1963, which received funding from the CCF after 1961. In 1960, his play *A Dance of the Forest* won a drama competition established by the CCF to mark Nigerian independence. This prize was first initiated by Michael Josselson, a CIA agent and administrative secretary of the CCF, in communication with Beier, and was run by *Encounter* with Stephen Spender, Mphahlele, and Beier as judges.[100] Soyinka was also one of the founding members of the Mbari Writers and Artists Club, which opened its premises in July 1961,[101] and his *Three Plays* was one of the first books to be issued by Mbari Publishing in 1963. Soyinka also took on a central role in the CCF-funded Conference of African Writers of English Expression at Makerere in Kampala in 1962, where he read from his own plays, and his poetry was reviewed by other participants. By 1963, Soyinka had a reputation as one of Africa's leading anglophone writers.

Thereafter, the Transcription Centre in London played a pivotal role in managing Soyinka's international reputation and visibility. Soyinka first met Dennis Duerden, director of the centre, at the Makerere conference. The following year, in May 1963, Duerden invited him to travel around Africa, to make eight half-hour television programmes with Lewis Nkosi, for a collaborative venture between the Transcription Centre and the National Television and Radio Centre of New York. From August to September 1963, Soyinka and Nkosi interviewed a number of writers, including Camara Laye, William Abraham, Chinua Achebe, Grace Ogot, David Rubadiri, Richard Rive, Vincent Kofi, and Ibrahim Salahi. These televised interviews and documentaries served to raise Soyinka's international profile. Indeed, one of the programmes was devoted specifically to Soyinka: he is shown producing a scene from one of his plays and is then interviewed by Lewis Nkosi about his work as a producer-playwright.[102]

Duerden worked closely with Rex Collings, Soyinka's editor at Oxford University Press, to help promote the playwright's work. As mentioned in

---

[100]   Coleman, *Liberal Conspiracy*, p. 203.

[101]   Letter, S. Charles to Soyinka, 7 March 1961, Box 518, Folder 10, IACF, Chicago.

[102]   Letter, Duerden to Soyinka, 23 May 1963, 18, TC/HRC.

Chapter 1, their offices were next door to each other in Dover Street, and their activities complemented each other: Collings published Soyinka's plays and poetry, while Duerden publicised them through radio programmes and newsletter articles, and organised theatre performances and filming of his plays. Collings published the first edition of the CCF prize-winning *A Dance of the Forests* (1963) and the comedy *The Lion and the Jewel* (1963) in his newly established Three Crowns Series; these were followed by *The Road* (1965) and *Kongi's Harvest* (1965). Soyinka became the flagship author of this new OUP series of African writing.[103] When Collings left OUP for Methuen in 1966, Soyinka left with him, and his first book to be published at Methuen was *Idanre and Other Poems* (1967). Collings continued to publish Soyinka's work in his eponymous imprint, beginning with his prison memoir, *Prisonettes: Poems from Prison* (1969). Even after the closure of the Transcription Centre, Duerden rented offices in the same building as Collings, in 6 Paddington Street, from 1969 to 1975.[104] Theirs was a very long-standing working relationship.

Duerden was committed to staging and filming productions of Soyinka's plays across Europe, at arts festivals and in the theatre. In 1964, Duerden invited Soyinka to help make twelve films for TV of modern African plays, with a 'mixed company of about 12 actors who might stay together for 2 years'.[105] However, Soyinka was hostile to the idea of a black British cast, wanting instead to have the play performed by Nigerian actors, and responded: 'I don't like it ... Tell me Dennis have you ever heard of an international theatre company of white actors ... a company like this, unified only by pigmentation is immediately hollow at the core'.[106] Duerden abandoned the idea, and instead requested the rights to film Soyinka's play *The Swamp Dwellers* for broadcast in the United States. Soyinka was offered a fee of £400 for the film,[107] with further payments for subsequent transmissions. Soyinka agreed to the terms, and wrote the

---

[103] Davis, *Creating Postcolonial Literature*, pp. 142–61.

[104] Letter, Platt to Duerden, 10 March 1969, 23.3, TC/HRC.

[105] Letter, Duerden to Soyinka, 2 January 1964, 18, TC/HRC.

[106] Letter, Soyinka to Duerden, 20 January 1964, 18, TC/HRC.

[107] Letter, Duerden to Soyinka, 27 April 1964, 18, TC/HRC.

narration for the play.[108] However, Soyinka was not involved in directing the film, and it became a major ordeal for Duerden over the next two years. It had to be re-cut to make the story clearer and the sound track more interesting, and he had to keep asking Farfield for more money to complete the project. The grand opening event in January 1965 had to be postponed for a year, and Soyinka advised Duerden to abandon the idea.[109] He persevered, but the film's final release in 1966 took place without fanfare or acclaim.[110] Despite Duerden's commitment to the production and promotion of Soyinka's plays, the playwright appeared fairly indifferent, even hostile, to his schemes.

Duerden also came into conflict with other members of the CCF over the promotion of Soyinka. The CCF organised the Berlin Arts Festival of 1964, and Soyinka was awarded a grant of £500 by Josselson to attend the festival with his Orisun Theatre group. Duerden sent the play script of *The Swamp Dwellers* to the conference organising committee, who rejected the play on the basis that it was peripheral to the interests of their audience.[111] Duerden wrote to Nicolas Nabokov, director of the festival, in protest, and asked if he could instead arrange for a private showing of *The Swamp Dwellers* film, but Nabokov upheld the decision of the selecting committee, and was discouraging about the film:

> I really doubt that it would have any impact at all at a time when we will have here live shows from Africa and thousand other events to which people will be running. But if you want to arrange a private showing, you had better take care of it yourself. Unfortunately I have not the time to bother with this kind of problem now.[112]

Although Duerden and the Farfield Foundation were staunch supporters of Soyinka, this view was not shared across the CCF as a whole.

[108] Letter, Soyinka to Duerden, 6 May 1964, 18, TC/HRC.
[109] Letter, Soyinka to Duerden, 19 March 1965, 18, TC/HRC.
[110] Letter, Duerden to Donald Stralem, 1 December 1965, 23.6, TC/HRC.
[111] Letter, Dr Bockermann to Duerden, 13 July 1964, 1.5, TC/HRC.
[112] Letter, Nicolas Nabokov, Berlin, to Duerden, 30 August 1964, 1.5, TC/HRC.

Duerden faced further difficulties in promoting Soyinka as Nigeria's national playwright at the 1965 Commonwealth Arts Festival in Cardiff and across the United Kingdom. He was in close communication with the director of the conference, to whom he wrote effusively praising Soyinka and his play *The Lion and the Jewel*.[113] Donald Stralem, director of the Farfield Foundation, awarded Soyinka a grant of £500 to help him with rehearsing in preparation for the festival, but, in the event, the plan was stymied by the Nigerian government, which selected Dúró Ládípò instead of Soyinka as their official playwright. The festival organisers then attempted to involve Soyinka in the conference by inviting him to serve on the film festival jury and to attend a meeting 'to 'establish an Association of Commonwealth Literature', but, in protest against the Nigeria government, Soyinka refused to be part of the official event, writing that the 'atmosphere' was 'too degrading'.[114] Soyinka insisted instead that the planned performance of *The Lion and the Jewel* be unconnected to the official Commonwealth Festival.[115] Duerden then helped to arrange for the play to be produced at London's Theatre Royal, in a production that ran for a whole month, from September to October 1965, in parallel with the main festival, and for Soyinka's poetry to be read at the Royal Court Theatre.[116] The Farfield Foundation funded the whole event, including Soyinka's expenses, and it was promoted through the other CCF-funded magazines. Despite being thwarted by the Nigerian government, Duerden, the Farfield Centre, and Rex Collings worked together to promote Soyinka as a leading African writer. Collings wrote a glowing advertisement of the two events for another CCF-funded magazine, *The New African*, describing Soyinka as 'Nigeria's leading playwright and ... undoubtedly one of the most exciting of the young dramatists writing in English anywhere in the world today'.[117]

Prison Campaign, 1965

The extent of CIA support for Soyinka was revealed during his period of imprisonment in 1965. During the post-electoral violence in Nigeria in

---

[113] Letter, Anthony Beech to Duerden, 11 July 1965, 18, TC/HRC.
[114] Telegram, Soyinka to Beech, undated [c.1965], 18, TC/HRC.
[115] Letter, Soyinka to Ian Hunter, 3 May 1965, 18, TC/HRC.
[116] Collings, 'First Commonwealth Arts Festival', p. 164. [117] Ibid., p. 164.

October 1965, Soyinka was jailed on a charge of robbery with violence, after forcing staff at the Nigeria Broadcasting Corporation at gunpoint to replace a tape of Chief Samuel Akintola's victory speech with a tape stating that the results had been rigged and announcing victory for the opposition. Initially, Soyinka was buoyant, believing that he would be released quickly. He wrote to Duerden:

> I write this from Ibadan police custody in whose tender care I've been for some 40 hours and seem likely to be for another 48 or so. Maybe you heard all the hue and cry. After 7 days 'under' I surfaced and am still 'assisting the police in connection with . . . ' etc. etc. The story of it shall occupy us when next we meet in wine.[118]

He welcomed the prospect of a major political uprising against the government, telling Duerden: 'I wish you were here now. Believe me, this is a great moment to be alive. I so badly needed reassurance that the people had not lost their will to resist wrong. There is hope yet'.[119] However, his hopes for an early release were dashed. He was imprisoned for much longer than he had first expected, was subjected to police violence, and went on a hunger strike.

Meanwhile, the Transcription Centre, the Farfield Foundation, and the CCF led a carefully orchestrated campaign for Soyinka's release. John Thompson wrote a letter to *The New York Times* asking them to draw attention to Soyinka's plight:

> Wole Soyinka, the distinguished Nigerian playwright, poet and novelist, has been jailed and, according to reports in British papers, has suffered from alleged beatings by police. . . . Without wishing to take sides on a matter sub judicae, a number of American writers have expressed concern over Soyinka's safety in a cable to Prime Minister Balewa. . . . The Farfield Foundation has made grants to assist in some of

---

[118] Letter, Soyinka to Duerden, 26 October 1965, 18, TC/HRC. [119] Ibid.

Soyinka's drama productions, and I regard him as a personal
friend. This, in addition to my concern for Soyinka as an
artist, is my interest in the matter.[120]

The New York Times duly published an article about Soyinka on 11
November 1965. Lewis Nkosi and Mel Lasky sent out fifty copies of a
press release, including a letter of protest signed by twenty-one
writers. Duerden then arranged with Amnesty International to send
their top barrister, John Mortimer, to Nigeria as an observer of
Soyinka's conditions in jail, and Amnesty arranged for him to write
an article for *The Sunday Times*, all paid for by the CCF in Paris.[121]
Duerden also wrote to the *Guardian* correspondent in Lagos, Walter
Schwarz, asking him to 'retain the best defence counsel available in
Nigeria to defend Wole Soyinka' and explaining that the 'Congress for
Cultural Freedom will meet the cost',[122] which in the event amounted
to £700.[123] Finally, in December 1965, Soyinka was acquitted. He
wrote to Duerden: 'Walter told me all you did. Thanks. I'll be writing
soon. Send me news'.[124] Duerden then wrote to Frank Platt, executive
director of the Farfield Foundation and a CIA agent, expressing
concern that Soyinka would get himself into trouble and damage the
reputation of the CCF:

It was good news about Wole – a reward for our efforts, but
I think he will soon get himself into trouble again. ... I
talked to John [Hunt] about it, and he said to ask you if it
wasn't possible to get him some kind of fellowship to get
him out of Nigeria for a year so that he wouldn't himself into

[120] Letter, John Thompson to Arthur Gelb, *The New York Times*, 5 November 1965, 18, TC/HRC.

[121] Letter, Ivan Kats, CCF Paris, to Peter Benenson, Amnesty International, 6 November 1965, 18, TC/HRC.

[122] Letter, Duerden to Walter Schwarz Esq., 8 November 1965, 18, TC/HRC.

[123] Telegram, Schwarz to Duerden, 10 November 1965, 18, TC/HRC.

[124] Letter, Soyinka to Duerden, 29 December 1965, 18, TC/HRC.

some more trouble. By calling himself 'Committee of writers for Individual Liberty' he is making some of it rub off
on us.[125]

While the expensive and extensive campaign for Soyinka's release demonstrates the extent of the CIA commitment to Soyinka, Duerden and John
Hunt's attempts to get Soyinka a fellowship in the United States suggest that
he was beginning to be considered a liability.

Soyinka's Tour of the United Kingdom, 1966

After his release from jail in 1966, Soyinka decided against going abroad,
explaining to Duerden, 'I don't think I will make a very good exile. A good
exile has to possess the kind of temperament which makes him unresponsive
to humanity in general. But as I said, I need a physical break for a period'.[126]
Instead, he decided to focus on his theatre group in Nigeria, the Orisun
Theatre Company, and visited New York in person to request financial
support from the Farfield Foundation.[127] He explained to Duerden his
desperation for the funding: 'I've had to clean out every living penny in
my possession and rob my salary to keep things going while we wait'.[128]

Soyinka decided that his company should go on tour in 1966, and
Duerden helped arrange for a number of productions of Soyinka's plays
across the United Kingdom. He managed to register the Orisun–Ijinle
Theatre Company in the United Kingdom, with Soyinka as its artistic
director, which would work closely with Soyinka's theatre company in
Nigeria.[129] Duerden also managed to secure Arts Council funding for
Soyinka's visit: a grant to cover the expenses of a UK tour to Leicester
University and Southampton University; a grant of £600 for a production of
Brother Jero at the Hampstead Theatre Club in June 1966, directed by Athol

---

[125] Letter, Duerden to Platt, 3 January 1966, 22.2, TC/HRC.

[126] Letter, Soyinka to Duerden, n.d. [*c*.25 October 1966], 18, TC/HRC.

[127] Letter, Barbara Knight to Duerden, 30 November 1965, 23.2, TC/HRC.

[128] Letter, Soyinka to Duerden, 31 January 1966, 18, TC/HRC.

[129] Letters, Duerden to Platt, 2 September 1966 and 11 November 1966, 23.2, TC/
HRC.

Fugard; and a subsidy of nearly £500 for the Ijinle Company's production of *The Lion and the Jewel* at the Royal Court Theatre.[130] Then, as a member of the organising committee, Duerden promoted Soyinka at the CCF-funded First World Festival of Negro Arts in Dakar in 1966. Duerden's time and funding were devoted almost exclusively to Soyinka in this period. He wrote to him, wryly, 'Keep yourself alive because I am putting more and more of my eggs in this particular basket and I can't do it without you'.[131]

During Soyinka's 1966 visit to the United Kingdom, Duerden was occupied full time with the organisation of the trip, including arranging television appearances with the BBC and Granada Television.[132] He grumbled to Platt: 'Wole arrived here on the 17th December and left on Christmas Eve and I was unable to concentrate for any period longer than one hour during that time'.[133] Duerden was particularly aggrieved that Soyinka showed no interest in the Orisun–Ijinle Theatre Company he had established, and was interested only in his own Nigerian theatre company, Orison: 'Wole merely sees Ijinle as a lever to help him bring Orisun over here. When he was asked by a journalist what he thought of the production, he said he was not interested in any theatre outside Nigeria!' Duerden concluded, 'I don't think we can run Ijinle simply as an appendage of Wole Soyinka and I very much want to find the work of other African playwrights we can do'.[134] Platt responded sympathetically, 'You certainly can't run Ijinle as an extra travelling theatre for Wole. You certainly sounded burnt by his remarks to the press. After all your incredibly hard work, I can't say as I blame you'.[135] The demands of promoting Soyinka and acting as his informal agent had started to take their toll on Duerden.

Tensions and Revelations

Following the first revelation of covert CIA funding of the Congress for Cultural Freedom by *The New York Times* in April 1966, there was pressure

---

[130] Letter, Duerden to Platt, 11 November 1966, 23.2, TC/HRC.

[131] Letter, Duerden to Soyinka, 25 October 1966, 18, TC/HRC.

[132] Letter, Duerden to Platt, 23 December 1966, 22.2, TC/HRC.

[133] Letter, Duerden to Platt, 28 December 1966, 22.2, TC/HRC. [134] Ibid.

[135] Letter, Platt to Duerden, 4 January 1967, 23.2, TC/HRC.

on the Transcription Centre to reduce its outgoings. Duerden came to the conclusion that his only option was to move from his expensive central London premises and to find cheaper, 'more approachable and more adaptable' premises in Paddington. He also proposed to reduce both the staff of the centre and the number of radio programmes.[136] However, these economies were still not sufficient, and in February 1967, Thompson warned Duerden that the future of the Transcription Centre was at risk.[137]

Duerden was obliged to place his relationship with Soyinka on a more commercial footing, and a lawyer advised Duerden that he would recover his expenses only if he received 30 per cent of Soyinka's royalties as commission, and that he should handle all Soyinka's work rather than just a part of it.[138] Soyinka was outraged by the proposal. writing, 'Your terms are impossible', and declaring that he would be looking for 'more permanent representation'.[139] Soyinka was at this time, in his own words, 'flat broke', as the Farfield Foundation had not sent him the funding he had come to depend on, and he had had to sack actors in his Orisun Theatre Company, as well as cancel plays that were in rehearsal. He wrote to Duerden, 'I'm busy rethinking the whole business from start to finish'.[140] Tensions came to a head when Duerden withheld Soyinka's £88 in royalties from the Royal Court production of *The Lion and the Jewel*, so that he could work out the commission he should take on behalf of the Transcription Centre.[141] Soyinka was outraged, and sent him a telegram, insisting that he forward the money directly: 'FOR CHRISSAKE DEDUCT AGENTS TEN PERCENT AND SEND BALANCE. SOYINKA'. He followed this up with a letter:

> It is ridiculous that I have to postpone or curtail my activities
> or even simply felt cramped about them because of the lack

---

[136] Letter, Duerden, 'Scheme Proposed for Transcription Centre 1967', 23.2, TC/HRC.

[137] Letter, Thompson to Duerden, 25 February 1967, 23.4, TC/HRC.

[138] Letter, Duerden to Platt, 24 January 1968, 23.3, TC/HRC.

[139] Letter, Soyinka to Duerden, 26 January 1967, 18, TC/HRC.

[140] Letter, Soyinka to Duerden, 3 February 1967, 18, TC/HRC.

[141] Letter, Helen Montagu, Royal Court Theatre, to Duerden, 6 February 1967, 18, TC/HRC.

of a few pounds which anyway I have lying somewhere. The money from Farfield hasn't come and I do not feel like sending a badgering telegram to Frank Platt. . . . This sort of thing affects me adversely and unnecessarily. . . . I do not mention my own personal eternal need for money because I assume you will take that for granted.[142]

Duerden sent Soyinka the full Royal Court fees, deducting no commission, but he explained that their business partnership was unsustainable on these terms: 'I suggest therefore that now the accounts have been settled we regard our partnership as concluded'.[143] Soyinka replied, acknowledging his debt to Duerden, but regretfully accepting the end of their business association:

It is unfortunate to discuss things in this way because it all implies that I do not appreciate the efforts which you made and have been making in literally every direction, or the facilities which I have been able to use at the Transcription Centre. But I think that we have reached the point where, for the sake of our future relationship, every attitude should be as unambiguous as possible, and your letter makes it impossible to escape a heavy atmosphere of accusation of me by you. . . . I think I'll simply stop there. The whole business is unfortunate.[144]

Duerden explained to Soyinka that all the promotional work he had previously carried out for Soyinka had been reliant on the grant from Farfield:

We have subsidised your work in many ways over a long period – principally in the amount of time and attention I have given to it. However we received a grant which enabled me to do it and I regarded it as one of the purposes for which

---

[142] Letter, Soyinka to Duerden, 28 February 1967, 18, TC/HRC.

[143] Letter, Duerden to Soyinka, 13 April 1967, 18, TC/HRC.

[144] Letter, Soyinka to Duerden, 12 May 1967, 18, TC/HRC.

we were given the grant. We have also derived some benefit
in the form of publicity from putting on your work. I am
extremely sorry that neither my staff nor I can afford to give it
the time and attention we have given it in the past particularly
as I have greatly enjoyed working with you.[145]

After a long pause, Soyinka acknowledged his letter, 'I got your last letter
and okay, we'll simply leave it at that and not prolong the argument'.[146]

Shortly before this, in April 1967, further revelations of the CIA investment in anti-communist operations worldwide were published in the US
magazine *Ramparts*, and the allegations were confirmed in an article by
former CIA officer Tom Braden in *The Saturday Evening Post* of May 1967.
This was evidently the moment that Soyinka became aware that he had been
covertly funded by the CIA via the Transcription Centre. In a later letter to
Platt, Duerden described a phone call he had made to Soyinka at this time:
'One of the most traumatic shocks of my life and I have had a great many
recently was virtually the complete reversal in Wole's attitude almost a year
ago when he learnt through a telephone call from my flat (which I paid for)
that your foundation was giving him a grant'.[147] The revelation evidently
resulted in a 'traumatic shock', from which Soyinka and Duerden's business
relationship never recovered. Duerden explained to Platt, 'the point is that
Wole and I agreed to part amicably and forget about our business association (and the two to three thousand pounds we spent on promoting him)'.[148]

Prison Campaign, 1967

In August 1967, Soyinka was once again imprisoned without trial for
attempting to broker a peace deal over Biafra. He remained in jail, in
solitary confinement, for the next twenty-six months. Despite Duerden's
recent fracas with Soyinka, and despite the beleaguered state of the
Transcription Centre, the CCF, and the Farfield Foundation at the time,
all three institutions united in campaigning for his release. Duerden

---

[145] Letter, Duerden to Soyinka, 23 May 1967, 18, TC/HRC.

[146] Letter, Soyinka to Duerden, 18 June 1967, 18, TC/HRC.

[147] Letter, Duerden to Platt, 24 January 1968, 23.3, TC/HRC.   [148] Ibid.

organised a letter to *The Times*, signed by several publishers, theatre directors, and authors protesting against his imprisonment and appealing for his release. He was in close communication with a representative of International PEN's Writers in Prison Committee, Peter Elstob, who visited Lagos in November 1967 to find out more about the situation, and to inform Amnesty International about Soyinka's case.[149]

Frank Platt also worked behind the scenes to arrange for Soyinka's release. He wrote to Duerden in January 1968: 'This is all very bad business about Wole. I am now trying to light a fire under UNESCO, and THE NEW YORK TIMES is always anxious for news and will always mention Wole's name in editorials. The pressure must be kept up'.[150] Platt also established close communications with Soyinka's Nigerian agent, Francis Oladele, visiting him in Nigeria and keeping in close contact with him thereafter about Soyinka's progress.[151] He also kept in touch with the British ambassador to the United States, and sent Duerden a telegram on 1 October 1968 that a 'medical officer saw Wole Kaduna prison early Sept. Found him well'.[152]

During Soyinka's imprisonment, the Farfield Foundation and the Congress for Cultural Freedom were both closed down following the funding scandal, but Platt continued at Farfield until 1969, distributing the remaining funds and working with the PEN Writers in Prison Committee in London.[153] He issued the final payment for the Transcription Centre in 1969,[154] and Duerden attempted for a few years to reposition himself as an 'intelligence service for African authors'. He renamed his company Transcription Features Services in March 1969 and took up new office premises with Rex Collings at 6 Paddington Street.[155] Meanwhile, the

---

[149] A. Codd, Southampton Branch of Amnesty International, to Duerden, 17 March 1968, and Duerden to Codd, 10 April 1968, 18, TC/HRC.

[150] Letter, Platt to Duerden, 12 January 1968, 23.3, TC/HRC.

[151] Letter, Platt to Saunders, 29 April 1968, 23.3, TC/HRC.

[152] Telegram, Platt to Duerden, 1 October 1968, 23.3, TC/HRC.

[153] Saunders, *Cultural Cold War*, p. 422.

[154] Letter, Platt to Duerden, 21 June 1968, 23.3, TC/HRC.

[155] Letter, Platt to Duerden, 10 March 1969, 23.3, TC/HRC. Duerden's financial problems continued, and he finally had to close the business in 1975 (see

relaunched International Association for Cultural Freedom (IACF) took up the mantle in campaigning for Soyinka's release, alongside International PEN and Amnesty International, sending regular protest letters to General Yakubu Gowon and keeping the story in the international press.[156]

Finally, when the Civil War came to an end in October 1969, Platt broke the news to Duerden: 'WOLE HOME SAFELY SENDS REGARDS NEW YORK TIMES RAN STORY TODAY WHOOPEE'.[157] After his release, Soyinka credited Duerden and his colleagues with keeping him alive: 'You people all worked like tigers – thanks for the efforts that probably saved my life'.[158] He then wrote a further letter: 'The wanderer is home again – thank you for your tireless efforts. A breathing space, just a little, and then to set about the necessary task of roasting the balls of evil men'.[159] Thus, during Soyinka's imprisonment, writers, publishers, newspapers, lawyers, and human rights agencies from Australia to the United States were successfully mobilised in his defence. At a time when the CCF was in a state of disrepute and dissolution, the re-formed IACF united in adopting Soyinka as its cause célèbre, thus promoting itself as an international guardian of intellectual and cultural freedom.

Conclusion

Allegations of CIA collaboration and 'cultural subservience' continued to plague Soyinka after the closure of the CCF.[160] In an interview with John Agetua in 1974, Soyinka referred to having been 'accused of being a CIA agent', adding that 'the CIA brush has been used very indiscriminately to smear everything literally that moves and that is opposed to the ideas of certain people'.[161] Despite this damage to his reputation, there is no evidence that Soyinka was aware of the CIA source of his patronage during the 1960s, or that the CCF or its affiliated institutions exercised a direct

Duerden to Debt Recovery Centre, Western Credit, 6 January 1975, 18, TC/HRC).

[156] Box 377, Folder 6, IACF, Chicago.
[157] Telegram, Platt (via Emily Hoyt) to Duerden, 9 October 1969, 23.3, TC/HRC.
[158] Letter, Soyinka to Duerden, 16 October 1969, 18, TC/HRC.
[159] Letter, Soyinka to Duerden, 21 October 1969, 18, TC/HRC.
[160] Benson, *Black Orpheus*, p. 285.
[161] Jeyifo, *Conversations with Wole Soyinka*, p. 44.

influence on his writing. Indeed, in his dealings with the Transcription Centre, he insisted on artistic control over his theatre productions, and he frequently contested or simply ignored many of Duerden's plans for the production and promotion of his work. Although Duerden was interested in promoting his work in the United Kingdom and the rest of Europe, Soyinka's main interest was always in his own Nigerian theatre company, Orison, and in Nigerian politics.

Yet, as Rubin argues, the CIA's influence was not limited to direct literary or political manipulation but was also exerted by a range of other activities.[162] Soyinka was prized and feted at arts festivals and literary conferences, and promoted through radio broadcasts and recordings and films of his plays. He was awarded grants for foreign travel and his theatre productions were funded and arranged across Europe and the United States. The close connections established between Duerden and London publishers, including Rex Collings, Andre Deutsch, and Heinemann, helped to get his work published, endorsed, distributed worldwide, and promoted at the highest level. Soyinka's interactions with the Transcription Centre reveal the exceptional degree of support that was given to Soyinka by the CIA and its affiliated institutions, which he took for granted, without questioning its source. As the CIA's leading African literary protégé, Soyinka was propelled to global prominence and designated Africa's foremost writer.

[162] Rubin, *Archives of Authority*, p. 59.

3 Nat Nakasa, *The Classic* and the Cultural Cold War

In July 1965, the 28-year-old South African journalist and literary editor Nat Nakasa fell to his death from the window of a seventh-floor New York apartment. He had recently left South Africa on a one-way exit permit to take up a Nieman Fellowship, a prestigious journalism scholarship, at Harvard University. Prior to that, from 1962 to 1964, he had been editor of *The Classic*, an international literary magazine based in Johannesburg. His rapid rags-to-riches rise and tragically young death led to his becoming, in the words of Lewis Nkosi, 'one of the principal mythical figures of that netherworld of Black South African writing'.[163]

The mythical status of Nakasa has been exacerbated by his mysterious connections with the CIA. The apartment he was staying in on the night he died belonged to Jack Thompson, executive director of the Farfield Foundation, which funded both *The Classic* and the Nieman Fellowships. The revelations provoked speculation. An early hypothesis was that this was a 'political assassination' by the CIA,[164] but these claims have been largely discredited, as several friends and colleagues have testified to Nakasa's increasing depression and despair in the weeks before his death, and to the fact that Thompson had taken him to his apartment to try to calm him down when he was threatening suicide.[165] Nevertheless, scholars and commentators continue to regard Nakasa as an unwitting pawn in the CIA's game, caught up in its covert Cold War operations, although there is little agreement about the exact nature of his involvement. Opinion ranges from that of the journalist Mlungisi Zondi, who, in the *Weekender* for 14 April 2007, describes 'soft, sensitive' Nakasa as an unwitting and naive recruit in the CIA covert right-wing and anti-communist operations[166]; while Piet Swanepoel, in his memoir about life inside the South African secret police, maintains that Nakasa was one of many left-wing activitists enlisted by the CIA to destabilise the

[163] Nkosi, 'Review', 475.   [164] Herdeck, *African Authors*, p. 272.

[165] Brown, *Native of Nowhere*, pp. 165, 168.

[166] Zondi, quoted in Acott, 'Tactics of the Habitat', p. 72.

Nationalist regime.[167] Nakasa's biographer, Ryan Brown, argues that he was a victim caught in between the 'vested and conflicting' anti-communist ideology of the United States and the South African states.[168] The covert nature of the CIA involvement in Nakasa's life, however, means that much is still unknown, and he continues to be an enigmatic figure in South African literary history.

While the relationship between Nakasa and the CIA has been subject to scrutiny, the involvement of the CIA in *The Classic* has received much less attention than other CIA-funded magazines such as *Black Orpheus* and *Transition*. This chapter draws on Nat Nakasa's papers at Wits University, which include rare evidence of the CIA's interventions in African publishing during his brief editorship of *The Classic* from 1961 to 1964, and which provide an important insight into the reasons for and implications of the cultural cold war in South Africa.

Origins

The origins of *The Classic* lay in a letter that Nakasa received from his childhood friend and former *Drum* magazine colleague, Lewis Nkosi, who wrote to him in November 1961 about a plan he had drawn up with Jack Thompson of the Farfield Foundation:

> Here is a plan we thought you might like! Jack wants to give you guys a small sum of money to help you start a cheap publication – a literary quarterly – coming out say four times a year. He would give you something like 100 dollars a month – or about £36 for organising it and printing. . . . We thought you and Can [Themba] might get together an interested group of African writers to organise a club for discussion and use the paper as mouthpiece of the group.[169]

Nakasa and Nkosi had first met Thompson, a former English literature academic at Columbia University, when he visited Johannesburg the

---

[167] Swanepoel, *Really Inside BOSS*, p. 144. [168] Brown, *Native of Nowhere*, p. 94.
[169] Nkosi to Nakasa, 30 November 1961, B1.11, A2696, Wits.

previous year as part of his literary tour of Africa, and he had subsequently arranged for Nkosi to receive a Nieman Fellowship at Harvard University.[170] This correspondence is enlightening, as it suggests that Thompson's principal plan for *The Classic* was not to establish it overtly for the publication of anti-communist propaganda but instead to create and support an association of black South African writers to establish a 'literary quarterly' as the 'mouthpiece' for 'an interested group of African writers'. Nakasa was well placed for this role because of his work with *Drum* magazine, and, as Themba had by this stage left South Africa for Swaziland, Nakasa agreed to take on the role of magazine editor alone.

This was, however, an unpropitious time to set up a literary magazine for black writers in South Africa. After the Sharpeville massacre of March 1960, a state of emergency was instituted. The African National Congress (ANC) and the Pan Africanist Congress (PAC) were banned in April 1960 under the Unlawful Organizations Act, and 18,000 arrests were made. Several South African magazines were shut down, and black South African writers were banned, silenced, and dispersed worldwide. The leading black magazine, *Drum*, had already stopped publishing political commentaries and moved away from short fiction, before it was eventually banned in 1965,[171] and other anti-apartheid magazines were also under state surveillance. The communist weekly *New Age* was eventually banned in 1962, and *Fighting Talk* was banned in 1963.[172] At this time, the CIA was funding a range of South African literary and political magazines, including the quarterly *Africa South*, which was banned in South Africa in 1960 after running for five years, and reissued from London as *Africa South in Exile*;[173] *Contrast*, edited by Jack Cope; *The New African*, established by Neville Rubin, Randolph Vigne, and James Currey in 1962; and the bulletin *South Africa Information and Analysis*, edited by Ezekiel Mphahlele and Lewis Nkosi.[174] Thompson's plans were thus in direct

[170] Benson, '"Border Operators"', p. 442.

[171] Ehmeier, 'Publishing South African Literature', pp. 115, 119.

[172] Lindfors, 'Post-War Literature in English', p. 53.

[173] Sandwith, 'Entering the Territory'.

[174] Ehmeier, 'Publishing South African Literature', p. 117.

conflict with the policies of the South African state, which was actively closing down any possible vehicles for black writers' self-expression or opposition to apartheid.

In this context, Nakasa struggled to assemble a community of writers for the new magazine. Thompson directed Nakasa to begin by establishing a trust into which Farfield could contribute funds, and assembling a board of trustees, but Nakasa reported back to him in July 1962 that he had had difficulties finding an 'unpaid, capable and sufficiently interested' team of people as the only other black South African on the board. Nakasa also experienced problems finding writers for the first issue, and he reported to Nkosi in January 1963 that he still needed 'four strong short stories' to start an issue 'worthy of a first number'.[175] Mphahlele and Nkosi stepped in to help him find material: Mphahlele offered his short story 'He and the Cat', and Nkosi 'The Promise', for the first issue of *The Classic*, and Nakasa was advised to travel to Cape Town to meet Richard Rive, another recipient of CCF funding, who introduced him to a group of local writers and artists, and gave him a 'bunch of stories', including Rive's own short story 'The Party'.[176] Thompson was concerned about the lack of progress, and Nkosi wrote to Nakasa complaining about the delay: 'It wasn't nice to get letters from New York, from Jack saying he hadn't had a word from you and didn't know what was happening. Anyway we can only hope that you are now going to be published at last'.[177]

Publishing The Classic, *No. 1*

The first issue of *The Classic* (Figure 6), published in May 1963, included an editorial comment by Nakasa that set out his mission statement to publish 'African writing of merit' that was the 'work of those writers with causes to fight for'.[178] Nakasa's article, 'Writing in South Africa', asserted his 'sense of grievance' about the 'feeling of rejection by the powerful hierarchy of the country's culture' and his view that literature in South Africa was a 'closed, hostile world'.[179] Despite this, it ended on a note of optimism: 'although

---

[175] Letter, Nakasa to Nkosi, 9 January 1963, B1.11, A2696, Wits. [176] Ibid.
[177] Letter, Nkosi to Nakasa, 3 February 1963, B1.11, A2696, Wits.
[178] Nakasa, 'Comment', *The Classic*, 1:1, p. 4.
[179] Nakasa, 'Writing in South Africa', p. 58.

Figure 6 *The Classic*, 1:1 (1963)

conflict exists on many levels between black and white, we are a single community with a common destiny and, therefore, requiring common ideals, moral values, and common national aspirations'.[180] The short stories and poems published in the first issue of *The Classic* demonstrate this concern to publish politically 'committed' literature.[181] It featured

[180] Ibid., p. 58. [181] Nakasa, 'Comment', *The Classic*, 1:1, p. 4.

predominantly the work of black South Africans, many of whom were Nakasa's former *Drum* colleagues. Nkosi's 'The Promise' recounts his memories as the first black director of a Durban-based advertising company, who has to endure the day-to-day racism of his white colleagues. Casey Motsisi's poem 'The Efficacy of Prayer' relates the tale of 'Dan the Drunk', who dies, has a pauper's funeral, and is 'dumped . . . into a hole to rest in eternal drunkenness', while Leslie Sehume's story 'I'm not a Tramp' tells the tale of a black man who is being hunted down on the false suspicion of stealing a diamond ring. After jumping into a lake to escape the dogs, he makes it to the other side of the shore but is eventually found by the search party and shot in the head. Can Themba's poem ' Dear God' is an invective against the idea of Christian patience and acceptance in the face of suffering, while his short story 'The Suit' recounts the aftermath of a marital affair, in which the betrayed husband insists, on pain of death, that his wife's lover's suit be 'treated with the greatest consideration', and that it should 'eat every meal with us and share all that we have'[182]; the strain and humiliation lead eventually to the woman's suicide. Richard Rive's short story 'The Party' recounts an evening in the life of a young coloured student, Manuel, who is persuaded to join a group of predominantly white students after a party to go into Cape Town, drink neat brandy, and paint political slogans on factory walls. At the end of the evening, he is arrested while his white friends escape, unpunished. Thus, the stories in the first issue are predominantly oblique critiques of the apartheid system, drawing attention to the predicament of black and coloured South Africans.

Nakasa received mixed responses to this inaugural issue. A reader called Andries Blose, who described himself as 'a writer in Zulu', wrote to Nakasa:

> I've just read through a copy of The Classic. I must say I was disappointed when I came to the last word. I craved for more of the same stuff. . . . I love the atmosphere that permeates the whole of the contributions in Volume One, particularly the short stories and poetry. There's that something about them that tells you in each case that there's a

---

[182] Themba, 'The Suit', p. 10.

> writer who knows my troubles, inhibitions, my joys, aspirations, failures, in fact who knows ME. Here's a man who relates episodes that happen in my waking hours but gives them the touch which makes me find the other side of even those things I'd thought I'd have to forget.[183]

For this reader, at least, the first issue managed in a unique way to express his 'troubles, inhibitions, . . . joys, aspirations, failures'. Wally Serote also registered his pleasant surprise at the contents of *The Classic*: 'it never occurred to me that you could write about Africans'.[184] The response of his CCF colleagues was more ambivalent. Mphahlele wrote: 'I am so glad you succeeded in bringing out *The Classic*. . . . The fiction is most uneven in quality, some of the things pretty slight, but it is a good and worthy beginning'.[185] Nkosi regarded it as a 'jolly good job for a start on the limited resources. We won't say anything about the quality of the writing yet'.[186] Thompson congratulated Nakasa – 'the Classic is damned interesting and I think you've done a great job'[187] – but encouraged him to avoid writing in a 'direct naturalist tradition' and making a political 'statement', and instead to adopt a more abstract aesthetic in publishing poetry that was less 'concerned with making a statement than with making a poem'.[188] This attempt to steer Nakasa towards the publication of apolitical literature exemplifies the CIA's interest in creating what Rubin describes as 'an illusion of the literary world outside of politics'.[189]

The Classic *and the Pan-African Network of the CCF*

Mphahlele was keen to bring *The Classic* under the auspices of the CCF, by aligning it with the other little magazines across the continent.[190] His aim

---

[183] Letter, Andries Blose to Nakasa, 21 November 1963, B1.14, A2696, Wits.

[184] Quoted in Brown, *Native of Nowhere*, p. 104.

[185] Letter, Mphahlele to Nakasa, 28 June 1963, B1.10, A2696, Wits.

[186] Letter, Nkosi to Nakasa, 23 July 1963, B1.11, A2696, Wits.

[187] Letter, Thompson to Nakasa, 3 July 1963, B3.2, A2696, Wits.

[188] Letter, Thompson to Nakasa, 13 August 1963, B3.2, A2696, Wits.

[189] Rubin, *Archives of Authority*, p. 18.

[190] Bush, *Publishing Africa in French*, pp. 187–8.

was to promote 'a strong triangle for exchange of material' between the magazines, including the exchange of copies and collaboration over their joint distribution. He encouraged Nakasa to contact the editors of the other literary magazines to ask them for material.[191] However, Nakasa's requests to Ulli Beier, editor of *Black Orpheus*, met with silence,[192] and his request to republish a story from *Black Orpheus* by Arthur Maimane was rejected.[193] In August 1963, Mphalele worked with Neville Rubin of *The New African*, to come up with 'a watertight fraternal agreement' to improve the sharing of materials between the magazines.[194] Rajat Neogy, editor of *Transition*, replied that he was in favour of sharing material so as to reach the 'widest possible audience', but he set out an elaborate list of complicated financial and legal terms on which material might be republished.[195] Nakasa, by contrast, was keen to avoid 'too many rules' and such a 'rigid arrangement'.[196] In the end, the three magazines failed to agree on a scheme for sharing material and Mphahlele's vision of a cooperative, pan-African literary community – supported by US patronage – failed to materialise.

Mphahlele and Nkosi continued, however, to offer support to Nakasa at a personal level. Mphahlele had worked closely with Nakasa when he was fiction editor of *Drum*, and continued to correspond with Nakasa, offering him career, financial, and editorial advice. He also wrote to Thompson, lobbying him to extend his support for *The Classic*. He explained to Nakasa in August 1963: 'I wrote to Jack before I left Paris suggesting that he push Classic financially so that it's kept going from strength to strength and becomes a talking point and a rallying point for writers through writers

---

[191] Letter, Mphahlele to Nakasa, 28 June 1963, B1.10, A2696, Wits.

[192] Letter, Nakasa to Beier, 31 January 1963, B2 Black Orpheus (and Transition), A2696, Wits.

[193] Letter, Beier to Nakasa, undated, B2 Black Orpheus (and Transition), A2696, Wits.

[194] Letter, Mphahlele to Nakasa, 5 August 1963, B1.10, A2696, Wits.

[195] Letter, Rajat Neogy to Neville Rubin, 12 August 1963, B2 Black Orpheus (and Transition), A2696, Wits.

[196] Letter, Nakasa to Neogy, 21 August 1963, B2 Black Orpheus (and Transition), A2696, Wits.

workshops'.[197] Nakasa relied on Mphahlele to contact African authors on his behalf,[198] and also to promote *The Classic* in the Chemchemi Cultural Centre.[199] In August 1963, he sent Nakasa 'In Corner B', which was about to be submitted to the East Africa Publishing House as the title story in a short story collection: 'Here is a story. You asked for it. But if you think it's all shit, please don't feel obliged to return it. I'll use it as manure at the right time'.[200] Nakasa accepted, proposing only that a paragraph of 'explanatory stuff about what happens when an African person dies' be deleted, as it was 'devoted to explaining custom rather like a sociologist would'.[201] Mphahlele agreed readily – 'You're right – scrap the whole of para 3. It's useless'[202] – and the story was eventually published in the third issue of the magazine. Nkosi also remained closely involved with *The Classic*. After the Nieman Fellowship ended, Thompson arranged for Nakasa to work for the Transcription Centre in London and funded him to go on a literary tour of Africa in August 1963, during which he sought out material for *The Classic*.[203] He also offered Nakasa regular support and editorial advice, suggesting that 'the magazine might toughen its critical sensibilities, so avoid being a "mutual admiration society"'.[204] These informal relationships with ex-*Drum* colleagues, sustained by CIA salaries, were more significant to Nakasa than the formalised CCF associations envisaged by Thompson and Mphahlele.

Whitewashing The Classic

In the face of new state censorship, Nakasa struggled to maintain *The Classic* as a multiracial magazine: 'neither African, nor non-white . . . simply a literary magazine for writers'.[205] He expressed his frustration in finding

---

[197] Letter, Mphahlele to Nakasa, 28 August 1963, B1.10, A2696, Wits.

[198] Letter, Nakasa to Mphahlele, 18 November 1963, B1.10, A2696, Wits.

[199] Letter, Mphahlele to Nakasa, 19 August 1963, B1.10 A2696, Wits.

[200] Letter, Mphahlele to Nakasa, 28 August 1963, B1.10, A2696, Wits.

[201] Letter, Nakasa to Mphahlele, 18 November 1963, B1.10, A2696, Wits.

[202] Letter, Mphahlele to Nakasa, 25 November 1963, B1.10, A2696, Wits.

[203] Letter, Nakasa to Nkosi, 14 August 1963, B1.11, A2696, Wits.

[204] Letter, Nkosi to Nakasa, 16 October 1963, B1.11, A2696, Wits.

[205] Letter, Nakasa to Matthews, 27 August 1963, B1.7, A2696, Wits.

suitable writers in a letter to the secretary of the Farfield Foundation: 'I am busy preparing and gathering material for the second issue of the paper. Sheer hell. Africa is not littered with frustrated Miltons eager to burst into the literary scene'.[206] As opportunities for black South African writers were closed down, Nakasa increasingly turned to white authors for contributions. He approached Doris Lessing in June 1963, and, although the letter took three months to reach her, she wrote back saying how much she liked the magazine, taking out a year's subscription and sending him two short stories,[207] 'Two Potters' and 'Outside the Ministry'. She worried that the latter, a satire of corruption in African politics, might be considered 'anti-African', although she added, 'I can't see this myself, unless to say that African politics must be similar to white politics is "anti-African"'.[208] Nakasa accepted the story, stating that he 'found nothing anti-African in it'.[209] In August 1963, just days before the second issue went to press, Nakasa wrote to Athol Fugard with an urgent request to publish an extract from his play about poor whites in Johannesburg.[210] Fugard replied:

> Under the circumstances – unless I wanted to be a real bastard – there is nothing for me to say except 'Go ahead and print'. In truth I am delighted that an excerpt from the play is to appear in The Classic. Your magazine has my most fervent moral support. I would however have appreciated an earlier notice of your intentions.[211]

After Nakasa's publication of a one-act extract of the play, Fugard wrote to Nakasa to express his delight in his handling of the play, thanking him for the payment ('A Godsend'), and telling him that he'd been contacted by a Broadway producer requesting a full copy of the play and who had

---

[206] Letter, Nakasa to Margaret R. Beels, 28 June 1963, B3.2, A2696, Wits.

[207] Letter, Nakasa to Lessing, 28 June 1963, B1.4, A2696, Wits.

[208] Letter, Lessing to Nakasa, 19 September 1963, B1.4, A2696, Wits.

[209] Letter, Nakasa to Lessing, 24 September 1963, B1.4, A2696, Wits.

[210] Letter, Nakasa to Fugard, 29 August 1963, B1.2, A2696, Wits.

[211] Letter, Fugard to Nakasa, undated, B1.2, A2696, Wits.

subsequently staged it.[212] Tom Hopkinson, former *Drum* editor, commented that the second issue of *The Classic* 'clearly has a great deal more "white content" than the first number'.[213] In featuring the work of established white writers, *The Classic* was shifting from its original aim to act as a mouthpiece for black South Africans.

From 1963, Nakasa exercised greater caution in his editing of the second and third issues of *The Classic*, in response either to Thompson's criticisms of the first issue, or to the more stringent censorship legislation that was being introduced. Of particular concern was the Publications and Entertainment Act, which was introduced in 1963, together with the creation of a new government board of censors, which meant that a publication could be banned if any part of it was deemed undesirable on political, religious, or sexual grounds.[214] When his friend Can Themba submitted a short story, 'Genuine Article', in June 1963, he warned Nakasa that 'It might be a good idea to ping them to a lawyer for whatever, but it's really not my station to tell my Ed. what and what not'.[215] Nakasa asked Themba to tone down the overt political message, stating 'although yours is a great story its success does depend on its subtlety', and asking him to delete the 'political soap box utterances' and make some fundamental changes to the characterisation.[216] Themba refused to make the changes and returned the unaltered manuscript to Nakasa with the comment, 'There's your bloody "The Genuine Article"'.[217] Nakasa replied:

> I notice that you have sent 'The Genuine Article' in its
> original form. You will recall that we discussed this story
> and you and I agreed up on a number of changes . . . At the
> moment I am against publishing your story as it is now
> however pushed for material I may be.[218]

[212] Ibid.

[213] Letter, Hopkinson to Nakasa, 5 December 1963, B2 Classic (Miscellaneous), A2696, Wits.

[214] Ehmeir, 'Publishing South African Literature', 111, 122.

[215] Letter, Themba to Nakasa, 13 June 1963, B1.13, A2696, Wits.

[216] Letter, Nakasa to Themba, 23 August 1963, B1.13 ba, A2696, Wits.

[217] Letter, Themba to Nakasa, undated, B1.13, A2696, Wits.

[218] Letter, Nakasa to Themba, 23 August 1963, B1.13, A2696, Wits.

Themba's response was that he should either 'approve and publish or reject and shoot back. You can comment your block off, but for halle-bloody-lulia's sake don't alter – not even a comma. These things are sacred to me'.[219] In the event, the story was never published.

Nakasa was equally cautious in his dealings with Arthur Maimane, another of his former colleagues from *Drum* who, in the early 1960s, was living in exile in Nairobi and working for Reuters. Nakasa repeatedly asked Maimane for material, and eventually the latter sent him the story 'The Mad Nest' with the warning, 'I hope it doesn't get you banned or anything like that'.[220] Nakasa initially thanked Maimane for his 'nice story' and offered him a fee of 15 guineas,[221] but after it had been typeset and was ready for press, Nakasa received legal advice to pull the story, as it was, in his words, 'too hot to handle' with its 'rather bold bedroom scene'.[222] He reluctantly withdrew the offer of publication, explaining to Maimane that the magazine had 'run into censorship problems': 'As we are anxious to remain in circulation it seems necessary to be cautious if only for a while . . . I am sorry to disappoint you in this matter, but this was completely outside my expectations'.[223] As a result, Maimane's 'The Mad Nest', like Themba's 'The Genuine Article', never saw the light of day.

Nakasa pondered how to create a more vibrant African literary culture in Johannesburg. The Assistant Editor of *Encounter* magazine, John Mander, met Nakasa on a visit to Johannesburg in 1963. Nakasa reported that 'he sounded me up about the possibility of opening a Mbari Writers' club in Johannesburg', and wrote to Thompson to ask what he thought of the idea.[224] Thompson was measured in his response, stating that the important thing was to get *The Classsic* more established: 'I don't know how many things you can do at once, but I feel sure that a successful magazine can be the foundation for other activities – but first the

---

[219] Letter, Themba to Nakasa, undated, B1.13, A2696, Wits.

[220] Letter, Maimane to Nakasa, 17 October 1963, B1.5, A2696, Wits.

[221] Letter, Nakasa to Maimane, 3 October 1963, B1.5, A2696, Wits.

[222] Letter, Nakasa to Mphahlele, 18 November 1963, B1.10, A2696, Wits.

[223] Letter, Nakasa to Maimane, 22 October 1963, B1.5, A2696, Wits.

[224] Letter, Nakasa to Thompson, 5 August 1963, B3.2, A2696, Wits.

magazine must be pushed along'. He was also a little uncertain about the prospect of funding the centre: 'about money for Mbari, I cannot promise anything myself, although when the magazine is going well I would be happy to entertain a proposal'.[225] Mphahlele was even more cautious about the idea:

> About a writer's workshop or rather a Mbari Centre, I'm sure you know best whether it can succeed in Joburg or not. Anyhow I think of Joburg as such a vicious place that acts both as a spur of things and as a killer. . . . when you have worked out some tangible scheme, I shall be happy to see it, if only because I'd like to keep in touch and help whenever I can.[226]

The lack of certain funding from Farfield, together with Mphahlele's assessment of Johannesburg as a 'vicious place' and a 'killer' of hopes served to curb Nakasa's ambitions. He abandoned the idea, recognising that he personally had no time to take this on, as 'there is far too much to be done getting the Classic out'.[227] But Nakasa explained to Thompson that *The Classic* suffered from a lack of literary community in South Africa: 'There is very little contact between The Classic and its contributors, who are all over the country and outside'.[228] The initial plans to create a literary hub were evidently proving problematic, and the initial dream of a thriving African literary community, with Johannesburg at its hub, was starting to fade.

Publishing The Classic, *No. 2*

The second issue of the magazine (Figure 7) moved away from the racial politics of the first issue. Nakasa's editorial comment focused on the need for literary quality and discernment in the face of the new 'scramble' for African literature:

---

[225] Letter, Thompson to Nakasa, 13 August 1963, B3.2, A2696, Wits.

[226] Letter, Mphahlele to Nakasa, 28 August 1963, B1.10, A2696, Wits.

[227] Letter, Nakasa to Thompson, 21 August 1963, B3.2, A2696, Wits. [228] Ibid.

Figure 7 *The Classic*, 1:2 (1963)

With publishers all over the world becoming increasingly interested in material from Africa, there has begun a vigorous, almost frantic, search for African writing. Welcome as this scramble may be, there are those of us who will be suspicious of its overall effects on the emergent writers on this continent. There is evidence already that much of the

> material which finds its way to print in this 'literary boom' really belongs in the waste-paper basket.[229]

His new concern was to be highly selective about the literature that was published – not to engage in a frantic 'search for African writing' but instead to select and promote work of high literary merit. The issue relied on the works of established white writers: in addition to the works by Fugard and Lessing, it contained a short story by theatre producer Barney Simon about two doves being released to freedom after their owner's death, as well as poems by the Senegalese president, Leopold Senghor. The work of only three black South Africans authors was published: a poem by Dubmore Boetie, which emphasised the humanity behind racial stereotypes; a black comedy by Benedict Wallet Vilakazi about prison life in South Africa; and a short story, 'The Riot', by Casey Motsisi, which inverted usual apartheid stereotypes by focusing on the unexpected act of mercy of an Afrikaner policeman and the savagery of a black crowd, who end up killing him. Although the texts were written in the traditional realist mode Thompson had criticised, it seems that Nakasa had taken his advice on board, for this time there was no direct political criticism of the apartheid system.

This issue gained approval from white authors and academics across South Africa. The new emphasis on literary quality and on art transcending politics was praised, for example, by Lionel Abrahams, who wrote to Nakasa: 'Because you know the reservations I felt after reading the first issue of "The Classic" I must let you know that No. 2 wipes them completely away. Congratulations! I think the new direction is the only right one for what can be our best literary magazine ever.[230]

Fugard also expressed his admiration for the magazine as a whole: 'Well Done Man! And I really mean this. A friend of ours down here whose opinion I think counts for a lot rates The Classic as the most exciting and significant quarterly on the SA literary scene'.[231] And Guy Butler of Rhodes

---

[229] Nakasa, 'Comment', *The Classic*, 1:2, 1.

[230] Letter, Lionel Abrahams to Nakasa, 19 November 1963, B2 Classic (Miscellaneous), A2696, Wits.

[231] Letter, Fugard to Nakasa, undated, B1.2, A2696, Wits.

University, Grahamstown, also sent him a letter of congratulation: 'It is a very important venture in South African literary history, and I wish it well'.[232] Under the joint influence of the South African state and the CIA, Nakasa was increasingly – albeit reluctantly – taking on a gatekeeping role, by censoring and sanitising the contents of the magazine. Nakasa's new determination to publish works of literary quality, to rely on prestigious white authors, and to self-censor literature rather than risk being banned, led to a more circumspect editorial approach, and also to greater recognition and approval among the white liberal literati in South Africa.

Distribution of The Classic

Distribution of *The Classic* was a constant problem for Nakasa, both internationally and within South Africa. Nakasa initially hoped that the Farfield Foundation would assist, asking Thompson if 'it would be feasible for us to send you about 100 copies for distribution by the Foundation, as we cannot, at present, afford to operate through an agency'.[233] Thompson replied that he could not take this number of copies, but did pay for a number of individual subscriptions.[234] Nkosi also tried to help distribute the magazine in London,[235] arranging for two bookshops to take copies and for Dennis Duerden of the Transcription Centre to take fifty copies,[236] but unfortunately they never arrived.[237] Nadine Gordimer asked friends all over America and Europe to take out subscriptions and to help distribute *The Classic*.[238] By these means, the magazine achieved a limited international circulation in the United States and the United Kingdom, but international sales were low.

---

[232] Letter, Butler to Nakasa, 28 September 1963, B2 Classic (Miscellaneous), A2696, Wits.

[233] Letter, Nakasa to Thompson, 24 June 1963, B3.2, A2696, Wits.

[234] Letter, Thompson to Nakasa, 3 July 1963, B3.2, A2696, Wits.

[235] Letter, Nakasa to Nkosi, 29 May 1963, B1.11, A2696, Wits.

[236] Letter, Nkosi to Nakasa, 23 July 1963, B1.11, A2696, Wits.

[237] Letter, Nakasa to Nkosi, 22 October 1963, B1.11, A2696, Wits.

[238] Letter, Nakasa to Nkosi, 29 May 1963, B1.11, A2696, Wits.

Within South Africa, Nakasa hoped to reach a new community of black readers, partly as a means of encouraging new black writers. He explained to Nkosi in October 1963:

> I have suddenly this idea that if we distribute fairly large number of copies of The Classic all over the country especially in the non-White townships we stand a chance of raising at least four new writers in a year. Such ideas can only be tried if I have time and am without the burden of free-lance journalism.[239]

However, the sales records show that Nakasa struggled to achieve this end: the initial print run was only 1,500 and sales in South Africa were modest. Nakasa relied on his management board members to sell copies and try to encourage subscriptions – for example, Gordimer also sent copies to friends all over South Africa – but distribution across the country was difficult.[240] In November 1963, James Matthews wrote to Nakasa: 'I must say that your second issue is taking a helluva long time to reach us at the Cape. I sincerely hope that "The Classic" is not going to take the same route many a literary magazine has travelled with as few appearances possible'.[241] Fugard similarly regretted that *The Classic* was not available in Port Elizabeth.[242] The subscriptions records reveal that the majority of sales in South Africa were, in fact, to white readers and racially segregated libraries. The other subscriptions were to commercial corporations, including *The Classic*'s other commercial sponsor, Anglo American Corporation, and in addition, Rupert Tobacco Corporation and Lever Brothers (SA) Limited. A few newspaper and book publishers also took out subscriptions, including Oxford University Press in Cape Town, the *Natal Mercury*, and *The Daily News*. The only record of a black South African institution taking out a subscription was Moroka High School, a Bantu Education

---

[239] Letter, Nakasa to Nkosi, 22 October 1963, B1.11, A2696, Wits.

[240] Letter, Nakasa to Nkosi, 29 May 1963, B1.11, A2696, Wits.

[241] Letter, Matthews to Nakasa, 18 November 1963, B1.7, A2696, Wits.

[242] Letter, Fugard to Nakasa, undated, B1.2, A2696, Wits.

school in Freetown. Of the forty-three individual subscriptions in South Africa, thirty-six were from white people. Despite Nakasa's hopes to distribute 'large number of copies of *The Classic* all over the country especially in the non-White townships', the magazine was circulated principally to a small white elite.

The limited support Nakasa received from Farfield and the CCF for the printing, sale, and distribution of *The Classic* suggests that reaching a large readership was not the CIA's main purpose. Instead, the principal objective of *The Classic* was evidently to extend the reach of the CIA's pan-African network of writers and intellectuals into South Africa.

Disillusionment and Escape

By August 1963 Nakasa was becoming increasingly disenchanted with literary publishing. He complained to James Matthews that 'like all other little magazines "The Classic" is permanently short of material',[243] and wrote to his former *Drum* colleague, Duke Ngiobo, 'The whole business of publishing has turned out to be a hair-raising affair, certainly not the fun and games I anticipated'.[244] Nakasa told Thompson that he was 'planning to leave the country on some grant or another',[245] and Thompson tried to persuade him to stay, encouraging him that he had 'done something great in starting The Classic' by bringing 'hope to your own people' and giving a 'solid demonstration of the qualities and abilities of your people'. Thompson secured him a personal stipend of $200 a month, initially for three months, but with the possibility of renewal.[246] This was in addition to the annual grant from Farfield, which by 1963 had reached $1,600.[247] In response, Thompson pressed Nakasa to continue his work in South Africa: 'We hope that this will allow you to cultivate your writers and perhaps meet with people in Cape Town and Natal to see if you can bring writers there into your group'.[248]

[243] Letter, Nakasa to Matthews, 27 August 1963, B1.7, A2696, Wits.

[244] Letter, Nakasa to Duke Ngiobo, 19 August 1963, B1.14, A2696, Wits.

[245] Letter, Nakasa to Thompson, 21 August 1963, B3.2, A2696, Wits.

[246] Letter, Nakasa to Nkosi, 22 October 1963, B1.11; Letter, Nakasa to Mphahlele, 18 November 1963, B1.10, A2696, Wits.

[247] Letter, Nimrod Mkele to Mr D. Bradford, 29 March 1963, B3.2, A2696, Wits.

[248] Letter, Thompson to Nakasa, 25 September 1963, B3.2, A2696, Wits.

In this period of intensifying political repression, Nakasa continued to seek opportunities to escape. After meeting Anthony Schulte of Simon & Schuster in Johannesburg in September 1963, he repeatedly wrote to him, asking him to help him 'get out of this hole', by assisting him in getting a Nieman Fellowship at Harvard.[249] He also wrote to Tom Hopkinson, the former editor-in-chief at *Drum*, now based in Nairobi, 'If I don't get the passport I'll take an exit and part finally with both South Africa and *The Classic*. I just want to go and breathe some fresh air before I'm too twisted to care about anything'.[250] With additional letters of support from Nadine Gordimer, Helen Suzman, and Allister Sparks, Nakasa was finally awarded a Nieman Fellowship. Although there is no mention in the archive of Thompson's role in securing this, the scholarship was covertly funded by the Farfield Foundation.[251] Refused a passport by the South African government, Nakasa's only option to leave was to take a one-way exit permit.[252] Nakasa then had protracted problems getting permission to enter the United States but, according to Dennis Duerden, John Thompson used his 'power and influence' to get Nakasa a work permit.[253] The American editor and publisher Jason Epstein, a close friend of Thompson's, explained in an interview with Saunders in 1994 that Thompson 'would offer fellowships to African scholars and intellectuals, and their governments would allow them to go on condition they never returned (they were glad to get rid of them). So what Jack was doing, without realizing it, was getting them exiled'.[254]

249 Letter, Nakasa to Tony Schuster, 3 December 1963, B2 Classic (Miscellaneous), A2696, Wits.

250 Letter, Nakasa to Hopkinson, 11 December 1963, B2 Classic (Miscellaneous), A2696, Wits.

251 Brown, *Native of Nowhere*, p. 109.

252 This was not the end of *The Classic*, however. After Nakasa's departure, Barney Simon and Casey Motsisi co-edited no. 4. After Motsisi left, Simon edited the next four issues until he left South Africa, and various guests edited the final four issues until 1971. Thereafter, Sipho Sepamla edited five editions of the *New Classic* from 1975 to 1978. In 1982 Jaki Seroke reinstated *Classic* for four more issues.

253 Duerden to Thompson, 5 April 1965, 23.4, TC/HRC.

254 Quoted in Saunders, *Cultural Cold War*, p. 427.

The subsequent difficulties Nakasa faced after he leaving South Africa have been recorded by his biographers: the problems he had getting his work published in New York, his shock and dismay at the racial discrimination he witnessed and encountered in the United States, his lack of financial security, and his intense anxiety about having no permanent right to remain in the United States, with no way of returning home.[255] He was, according to Keaney, a man 'broken by exile'.[256] Nakasa's vision of America as a place where he could 'breathe some fresh air', was, in the end, a delusion.

Conclusion

The argument that Nakasa was a pawn in the CIA's game, and that *The Classic* was a vehicle for CIA propaganda, is not in fact supported by the evidence. Although Thompson had some success in steering Nakasa's editorial policy towards an apolitical, conservative agenda, and in ensuring that the magazine operated within certain political parameters, he exercised no power of veto over the contents of *The Classic*, and the magazine was by no means a vehicle for anti-communist propaganda. Indeed, as far as the South African government was concerned, many of its authors, including Mphahlele, Themba, and Nkosi, were later banned by the South African government under the Suppression of Communism Act,[257] and, at the point Nakasa left South Africa in 1964, the police were preparing to ban him as a communist for 'stimulation of the spirit of hostility between the whites and non-whites'.[258]

Ultimately, Thompson and Mphahlele's ambition to establish a multiracial community of South African writers, with *The Classic* as its mouthpiece, proved naive and unsustainable. Their vision of cooperation was not shared by the various editors of the African literary magazines, or within South Africa. For Nakasa, the patronage extended by the CIA – his appointment as an international literary editor, his escape on a one-way exit pass from South Africa, and his receipt of a prestigious journalism

---

[255] Brown, *Native of Nowhere*, pp. 126–69.

[256] Keany, 'Sophiatown Shebeens', p. 127. [257] Chapman, *Drum Decade*, p. 185.

[258] Brown, *Native of Nowhere*, p. 94.

fellowship at Harvard – led not to his achieving the American dream but to his untimely death. The literary strategies of the American and South African states in their respective wars against communism were in direct conflict with each other, with disastrous results for Nat Nakasa, who was caught in the crossfire.

4 'The Displaced Outsider': The Publishing Networks of Bessie Head

After the publication of her second novel, *Maru*, in 1972, Bessie Head wrote to her editor Gordon Graham at Gollancz publishers, reflecting on the American and British reviews of the book: Something tortures me slightly. I am dependent on an audience, seemingly hungry to comprehend 'the real Africa' and over-eager to take a writer as the epitome of everything African. How much I am the displaced outsider, I alone know . . . I am discomforted by the title "genuine African writer"'.[259] She remarked on the contradiction between the critics' perception of her and her actual circumstances: the gap between her reputation as a writer who expressed universal truths about 'the real Africa', and her own position as a 'displaced outsider', as a mixed race, illegitimate South African exile and stateless refugee. The paradox of this situation was a recurrent theme in her letters to her publishers during her early writing career.

Eileen Julien argues that Head's first two novels, *When Rain Clouds Gather* and *Maru*, are prime examples of the 'extroverted African novel', literature that is 'turned outwards', and that is marked by archetypal, allegorical, and 'emblematic qualities' but disconnected from the interests of readers in Africa.[260] She maintains that success in the global literary marketplace for the African novelist is contingent on the novel's ability to 'cross borders' and appeal to national elites rather than local readers, and that '"the African novel" is recognised as such precisely because it is characterised by extroversion and engagement with what is assumed to be European or global discourses'.[261] Her contention that the form of the novel in Africa bears the mark of unequal international literary power relations is based on the assumption that many African novelists write specifically for their European and American publishers and readers. Revisiting her theory in 2018, Julien explains that conditions of extroversion depend on multiple factors including language, place of publication, and possible publics, and

---

[259] Letter, Bessie Head to Giles Gordon, 22 January 1972, Box A, Folder 24, Item 34, BHP/KMM.

[260] Julien, 'Extroverted African Novel', pp. 681, 685, 696. [261] Ibid., pp. 689, 685.

she maintains that it is the reception of a novel – how it is received by the global literary establishment and by readers across continents including Africa – that accounts for its status in the world market as an 'African novel'.[262] This chapter charts Bessie Head's early writing career, from 1962–72, to consider the impact of international publishers and international reading publics on her work and question whether these 'practices of production and reception' led to her novels' 'extroversion'.[263]

As a relative outsider, on the periphery of the CCF literary network in Africa, Head relied on forging her own epistolary networks with commercial publishers in Britain and America for her literary career, and I examine her engagement with three interconnected publishing communities. First, Head's early involvement with the CCF-funded magazine, *The New African*, secondly, her encounter with the New York publisher of *When Rain Clouds Gather* (1971); and, thirdly, her relationship with the British publisher of *Maru* (1972). With reference to Head's correspondence with her editors and her London-based literary agent, I examine whether they imposed specific conditions on her work, and review her reaction to her publishers' and readers' expectations of a 'genuine African writer'.

Bessie Head and The New African

In the early 1960s, Bessie Head became connected to the CCF through the Cape Town magazine *The New African*. This anti-apartheid political and cultural magazine was established in January 1962 by Randolph Vigne, Neville Rubin, and James Currey,[264] and Bessie Head's husband, Harold Head, received a small sum for managing the magazine's administration and circulation.[265] Her work was published alongside that of her former *Drum* colleagues Dennis Brutus, Lewis Nkosi, Bloke Modisane, Ezekiel (later Es'kia) Mphahlele, James Matthews, Richard Rive, and Alex La Guma. In

---

[262] Julien, 'The Extroverted African novel, revisited', p. 376. See Suhr-Sytsma, 'The Extroverted African Novel and Literary Publishing' for further discussion of Julien's theory.

[263] Julien, 'Extroverted African Novel', p. 681.

[264] Vigne and Currey, *The New African*, p. 8.

[265] H. Head, 'Piet de Vries', pp. 5–6.

fact, Head was the only non-white South African female writer for *The New African*. The magazine was distributed principally to a small, predominantly white, liberal audience in South Africa and the United Kingdom. Although *The New African* was initially self-supporting, after Rubin attended the Makerere Conference of African Writers of English Expression in 1962, Mphahlele made arrangements for the Farfield Foundation to award the magazine an annual grant.[266]

The CIA source of the funding was initially unknown to the magazine editors. Vigne and Currey were assured that, although the charitable foundations behind the CCF were unnamed, they were 'highly respectable', particularly as they were the funders of *Encounter*. Only after the funding source was revealed in 1966 did the editors become aware of its CIA backing. Vigne insisted that the money had been awarded unconditionally, and in his editorial of December 1966 he wrote, 'We have been blessed since 1962 with financial support, mainly from the Congress for Cultural Freedom, which has on no occasion tried to influence our policy'.[267] They conceded, in retrospect, that the magazine, with its liberal, anti-communist stance, had played a part in the Cold War: 'We might not like it but we were all . . . forced to take sides in the Cold War'. Ultimately, they considered the CIA patronage of African literature to be 'inspired' and 'a vital factor in the rapid growth of African literature in English'.[268]

As a struggling journalist in Cape Town from 1962 to 1964, whose career as a writer was achieved against the odds, Head relied on *The New African* for the publication of her early work. A mixed race, illegitimate woman living in conservative and racially segregated South Africa, she was, according to her friend Tom Holzinger, 'an outcast from the moment of her conception'.[269] Yet, *The New African*, with its non-racial editorial policy, provided a vital platform for Head's development as a writer. Her first poem, 'Things I Don't Like' (1962), is written from the perspective of a disaffected, violent black man in South Africa.[270] Her first article in *The New*

---

[266] Vigne and Currey, *The New African*, p. 8.   [267] Vigne, 'Come What May', p. 1.
[268] Vigne and Currey, *The New African*, pp. 5, 23.
[269] Personal interview with Tom Holzinger, Serowe, 30 May 2019.
[270] Head, 'Things I Don't Like', p. 10.

African, 'Let Me Tell You a Story Now', reflects on her difficulties in forging a career as a writer: 'two unpublished manuscripts. One got lost in the post. The other got lost among the papers and rubble on a publisher's desk . . . It was a hotch-potch of under-done ideas, and, monotonous in the extreme'. She resolves, 'Whatever my manifold disorders are, I hope to get them sorted out pretty soon because *I've just got to tell a story*'.[271] Thereafter Head wrote articles that document the poverty-stricken lives of black and coloured communities under apartheid. 'A Gentle People' describes the 'warm, uncommitted "Coloureds"' of the Cape;[272] the short story 'Snowball: A Story' tells of the life and sudden death at sea of an ex-thief from District Six in Cape Town;[273] and 'The Isolation of Boeta L' describes the desolation of the Atteridgeville township near Pretoria.[274] In her early work for *The New African*, Head began to take on the role of a reporter, bearing witness to the conditions of racially excluded communities and marginalised individuals in South Africa for a predominantly white, liberal reading public.

The New African was forced to move from Cape Town to London. As censorship intensified in South Africa, state surveillance increased and the magazine was subject to police harassment. Vigne was banned in March 1963, on suspicion of sabotage and for anti-apartheid publishing, and was finally forced to leave South Africa in July 1964; he was soon followed by James Currey, who had assisted him in his escape. The third *New African* editor, Neville Rubin, had already left South Africa to take up a new position at the School of Oriental and African Studies in London. From March 1965, the magazine was published from London. Vigne continued to edit it and also to carry out work for the CCF.[275] The magazine was banned in South Africa in June 1965, and was circulated under different names; readers were instructed to destroy it after reading for fear of prosecution. As a result, it struggled to maintain its South African readership, and its circulation was confined mainly to British readers.[276]

---

[271] Head, 'Let Me Tell You a Story Now', pp. 8, 10.

[272] Head, 'A Gentle People', p. 169.   [273] Head, 'Snowball: A Story', p. 100.

[274] Head, 'The Isolation of Boeta L', p. 28.

[275] Vigne, 'Wole Soyinka Case', 4 November 1965, Box 296, Folder 2, IACF, Chicago.

[276] Vigne and Currey, *The New African*, p. 21.

Shortly before Vigne and Currey left South Africa, Head was also forced to leave on a one-way exit permit for Bechuanaland (now Botswana). Determined to continue her career as a writer, she embarked on a long personal correspondence with Vigne, and continued to send him regular work for *The New African*, despite feeling 'disastrously cut off' from any writing or publishing centre.[277] Vigne published the majority of the pieces without asking for any corrections. As she explained to a mutual friend, 'I work so well with him when I do pieces for the New African and I can't think of my writing life without Randolph having a big say in it'.[278]

Head's early articles reflected on the extreme difficulties of life in Bechuanaland, a British protectorate on the brink of independence. 'For Serowe, a Village in Africa', published in the December 1965 issue of *The New African*, dwells on the deprivations of daily life in the village: 'Everybody survives on little and there may be the tomorrow of nothing. It has been like this for ages and ages – this flat, depressed continuity of life; this strength of holding on and living with the barest necessities'. She concludes, 'I am like everyone else – perplexed, bewildered and desperate'.[279] Her next article was 'Looking for a Rain God', published in April 1966, which recounts a local news story about a group of villagers who come together during a terrible drought to sacrifice two small girls in the village as an offering to the rain god:

> the men were beyond caring and agreed with the old man that the two little girls should be sacrificed to this terrible rain god. Then the crops would grow . . . Since the women were half demented by this time and the intense heat was even destroying the wild devil thorn on which the goats grazed, they too agreed to the sacrifice of the children.[280]

This tale of 'half demented' villagers and child sacrifice is the bleakest of Head's articles. Her new role in *The New African* had become that of foreign

---

[277] Vigne, *Gesture of Belonging*, p. 29.

[278] Letter, Head to Cullinan, 5 June 1969, 2015.176.1.38, Amazwi, Grahamstown.

[279] Head, 'For Serowe, a Village in Africa', p. 230.

[280] Head, 'Looking for a Rain God', p. 65.

correspondent from southern Africa, reporting on the extreme problems of the region.

In her letters to Vigne, Head reflected on the irony of her situation: a refugee and outsider in Botswana who was, at the same time, a spokesperson for southern Africa. In January 1966 she wrote to Vigne, 'After all, I'm such an isolated goddam outsider trying to be an African of Africa. Believe me – it's painful and just guesswork – but such desperate guesswork. . . . I guess, I grope I guess at some goddam unfathomable life I'm not really a part of. But one does not know where one belong's.[281]

While Head struggled to reconcile this paradox of 'trying to be an African of Africa' while not knowing 'where one belongs', she decided to continue writing about her immediate situation. In August 1966, she wrote to Vigne: 'How do you write about nothing. You must make yourself part of the life of the country, even if it's painful and confused'.[282] In her final article for *The New African*, published in the August 1968 issue, Head wrote of her 'capacity as an underdog to identify myself with all peoples in the world living under such conditions', deciding in the end that it was her status as an 'underdog' that qualified her for the role of a spokesperson for southern Africa.[283]

While *The New African* was a vital means of launching Head's writing career and positioning her as an up-and-coming African writer, it could not be relied on as a source of income. Vigne continued his unwavering support of Head in *The New African* until the magazine finally came to an end in November 1969. Its penultimate issue (no. 52) in May 1969 featured Head as a leading African writer, with her photograph on the front cover, alongside Ama Ata Aidoo, Mbelle Sonne Dipoko, and Aimé Césaire. However, the magazine had struggled financially after CCF funding ceased in December 1966,[284] and Head's income for her contributions, always meagre, became even more sporadic. By 1968, Vigne was obliged to write to Head explaining, 'The NA has nothing but debts at present' and apologising for the delay

[281] Letter, Head to Vigne, 16 January 1966, quoted in Vigne, *Gesture of Belonging*, p. 24.
[282] Letter, Head to Vigne, 9 August 1966, quoted in Vigne, *Gesture of Belonging*, p. 38.
[283] Head, 'God and the Underdog', 48.
[284] Vigne and Currey, *The New African*, p. 23.

in paying her for her work. Head's writing was also published in three other CIA-funded magazines, *Transition*, *Encounter*, and later *The Classic*, but she never benefited from the direct financial patronage and travel opportunities that many of her South African counterparts received, for example Brutus, Nkosi, Modisane, Mphahlele, Matthews, Rive, and La Guma.[285] As a result, Head was forced to turn to New York and London commercial publishing firms to sustain her writing career.

The Publication of When Rain Clouds Gather

Head's connection with New York book publishers came about entirely by chance. Jean Highland, literary editor of Simon & Schuster, approached Head out of the blue to invite her to write a novel, after reading her article 'The American Woman' in the *New Statesman*. Head explained the situation to her friend and benefactor Pat Cullinan: 'The main thing is I did not find Simon & Schuster. A woman editor there found me. That it was love at first sight was lucky for me'. Highland invited Head 'to get busy on a book', sending her an advance of £80, and then helping her edit the manuscript, with two other editors, Bob Gottlieb and Pat Read, with whom Head had a 'powerful friendship such as I have never experienced in my life before'.[286] She described how 'Bob pulled out pages of the typescript of "RAIN CLOUDS" and said "re-write that" with a sure hand. He pulled out everything exactly where I had slowed down and had sloppy, slip-shod thoughts. I appreciated it'.[287] The editorial correspondence for *Rain Clouds* has not survived but in her retrospective reflections on the editing process, Head described it as a 'mystical' meeting of minds, in which 'the wave-length was so good'.[288] She also praised Pat Read and Jean Highland's editing work: 'Jean and Pat gave me [more] affection than I have ever had in my life'.[289] Such collaboration with her editors was, in Head's view, essential to her creativity: 'Whatever

[285] Gray, *Free-lancers and Literary Biography*, p. 162.

[286] Letter, Head to Cullinan, 4 June 1969, 2015.176.1.38, Amazwi, Grahamstown.

[287] Letter, Head to Machin, 10 June 1970, Box B, Folder 60, Item 28, BHP/KMM.

[288] Letter, Head to Machin, 11 February 1970, Box B, Folder 60, Item 27, BHP/KMM.

[289] Letter, Head to Machin, 18 June 1969, Box B, Folder 60, Item 11, BHP/KMM.

happens to RAINCLOUDS in America I know I have real friends there ... I really have to be loved before I can produce, the same way the earth has to be irrigated before things grown there'.[290]

The book was published by Simon & Schuster in 1968, and was successful in the United States. By May 1969, it had gone into a second print run of 2,500 further copies,[291] and by 30 September 1969, 4,000 hardback copies had been sold. Highland, who had moved to Bantam Books, then managed to persuade Bantam to buy the paperback rights for the novel for $6,000,[292] of which £1,000 was paid to Bessie Head (£800 after her agent's deductions).[293]

The publisher attributed the novel's success to its appeal to young black readers in black studies programmes. One of Head's editors, Pat Read at Simon & Schuster, explained to Head that these readers wanted 'to know more about life in foreign lands, particularly in Africa':

> As you probably know, there is a strong movement in this country among young black Americans to learn more about Africa and their heritage from your continent. Your book is especially well suited to give a picture of life as it really is in a newly independent country. I like the idea of your serving as a link between our countries, and I hope you do, too.[294]

Head was marketed by her New York publishers as an archetypal African who painted 'a picture of life' in Africa, and enabled readers to 'learn more about Africa and their heritage'. As a book that physically crossed borders, and that enabled black American school children to 'glean information about "Africa"', *Rain Clouds* bore the archetypal marks of an 'extroverted novel'.[295]

---

[290] Letter, Head to Cullinan, 4 June 1969, 2015.176.1.38, Amazwi, Grahamstown.

[291] Letter, Patricia Read to Head, 12 May 1969, Box A, Folder 111, Item 2, BHP/KMM.

[292] Letter, Highland to Head, 19 June 1969, Box A, Folder 43, Item 4, BHP/KMM.

[293] Letter, Machin to Head, 24 June 1969, Box B, Folder 60, Item 12, BHP/KMM.

[294] Letter, Patricia Read to Head, 12 May 1969, Box A, Folder 111, Item 2, BHP/KMM.

[295] Julien, 'Extroverted African Novel', p. 689.

Rain Clouds was also successful in Britain, where it was published by the London firm Victor Gollancz. Head had contacted the Gollancz editor Giles Gordon three years earlier, asking if he would like to see her short stories and explaining the difficulty of her circumstances: 'I am in in a pretty ghastly situation. I am a stateless person from South Africa and have spent the best part of a year wandering about unemployed'.[296] Although Gordon declined to publish the short stories, he seized the chance to co-publish the British edition of *Rain Clouds*, which came out in May 1969. The initial 1,107 hardback copies sold out quickly, and 2,000 additional copies were reprinted.[297] Throughout 1969, the book sold at a rate of about fifty per week,[298] and Head received a 10 per cent royalty on the first 2,500 copies.[299] Penguin then made an offer to publish the British paperback edition, and Head reported to her literary agent, David Machin of A. P. Watt & Sons, that she was 'very pleased with the Penguin offer. I can't help feeling that RAIN CLOUDS is getting very upper class treatment'.[300] The financial rewards for Head were considerable: the money she received from the sales of the hardback and paperback, including the sizeable advances for each, enabled her to establish a life as an independent writer. She wrote to Machin that she was finally 'supporting myself with writing, which I feel is really my life's work'.[301]

A year after the publication of *Rain Clouds*, Head wrote to Graham, reflecting on the contradictory consequences of the publishing experience:

> I am despised by many people, especially Africans … It affects the white people too. They try to shout me down, after they have bought my book. I really don't dig these kinds of people at all. They only hurt me when I am broken down in health and mind but some of the greatest pleasure in my life has been corresponding with some really coherent people in

[296] Letter, Head to Gordon, October 1966, Box A, Folder 24, Item 1, BHP/KMM.
[297] Letter, Gordon to Head, 13 May 1969, Box A, Folder 24, Item 8, BHP/KMM.
[298] Letter, Gordon to Head, 8 July 1969, Box A, Folder 24, Item 11, BHP/KMM.
[299] Letter, Machin to Head, 5 January 1968, Box B, Folder 60, Item 1, BHP/KMM.
[300] Letter, Head to Machin, 28 April 1969, Box B, Folder 60, Item 7, BHP/KMM.
[301] Letter, Head to Machin, 10 July 1970, Box B, Folder 60, Item 28, BHP/KMM.

America and England. . . . I involved them in Africa in my own way and forced them off the white man's horse and in return, they forced me to keep very alert mentally.[302]

After the publication of *Rain Clouds*, Head regarded herself as more connected to the 'coherent people in America and England' than she did to the local Botswanan people. She felt that she was 'despised by many people, especially Africans', accusing them of shouting her down after reading her book, when she was already 'broken down in health and mind'. The consequence of publishing a successful 'African novel' with 'appeal across borders' was a sense of alienation from her local readers.[303]

Writing for the American Public

Head struggled to recreate this supportive international publishing community for her second novel. She sent Jean Highland an outline of her new, philosophical, book 'Patterns', which was based on the 'sudden illumination' that when people 'respect each other . . . the way is open for the brotherhood of man and the removal of poverty and suffering', but was met by a long silence. Baffled, Head wrote to Machin, her literary agent in London, asking if he might know the reason for this, and he ventured that it was likely to be because of the religious themes of the book: 'people who make up the book world in Western Europe and North America' are 'very sceptical about any non-historical writing which smacks of belief in a Christian-type God and of mysticism'.[304] Three months later, Head received a brief reply from Highland that the work was 'so difficult for her'.[305] Bitterly disappointed, she abandoned the novel.

---

[302] Letter, Head to Gordon, 19 November 1970, Box A, Folder 24, Item 19, BHP/ KMM.

[303] Julien, 'Extroverted African Novel', pp. 676, 681.

[304] Letter, Machin to Head, 19 February 1969, Box B, Folder 60, Item 3, BHP/ KMM.

[305] Letter, Head to Machin, 19 August 1969, Box B, Folder 60, Item 18, BHP/ KMM.

Soon afterwards, Head was approached by the children's editor Anne Stephenson at Simon & Schuster, who asked if she would be interested in writing a new novel, explaining that Head was '*exactly* the kind of writer we need to write for adolescents and teenagers', and inviting her to 'write another wonderful story like WHEN RAIN CLOUDS GATHER, but from a young person's point of view' and only half the length.[306] Somewhat offended about being categorised as a children's author, Head complained to her agent, 'The lady insulted me by suggesting that I was especially born for her department. My sentence construction is simple but I am sure you will agree with me that my outlook on life is not child-like'. But Machin persuaded her to consider the proposition,[307] and Head agreed with him that writing this short novel might release her from her 'dead end' and 'solve the problems of my cul de sac'.[308] Although she accepted Stephenson's invitation, she resisted the idea of writing a children's book: 'Of course it has never occurred to me to write for children ... I would not like to promise to produce material directed at a particular audience'. She proposed instead to send Stephenson the manuscript and let her decide whether it fitted the bill.[309] Head began writing immediately, and reported to Machin that she was 'working like a steam roller, at full speed ... I needed the push. I have been dithering too much ... At the moment I am as happy as a bee, working, working'.[310] She managed to complete the manuscript of *Maru* within a month.

Maru is a novel about racial exclusion and prejudice in Botswana. The protagonist of *Maru*, the schoolteacher Margaret, is a Khoi San female teacher – a *maswara*, or 'bushman' – who is despised and ostracised by her local community. Head explained to Machin that the subject matter was close to her son's experience in Botswana: 'A lot of the material in

---

[306] Letter, Stephenson to Head, 17 July 1969, Box A, Folder 111, Item 3, BHP/KMM.

[307] Letter, Machin to Head, 8 August 1969, Box B, Folder 60, Item 17, BHP/KMM.

[308] Letter, Head to Stephenson, 24 July 1969, Box A, Folder 111, Item 4, BHP/KMM.

[309] Ibid.

[310] Letter, Head to Machin, 30 July 1969, Box B, Folder 60, Item 16, BHP/KMM.

the present work is based on what happened to my little boy last year when he was assaulted, and also what happened to me'.[311] She explained that

> Neither my son nor I look genuinely African types because my mother happened to be a white woman while my father was an African man. This was very soon pointed out to my son at school. The main thing is that an inferior tribe here happen to have the same complexion as I, which is yellowish . . . I was also informed that I was a bushman, a part of the inferior tribe.[312]

In writing *Maru*, Head returned to her self-appointed role as a spokesperson for outcasts and underdogs in southern Africa.

Head sent a complete manuscript to Anne Stephenson at Simon & Schuster in August 1969, and a further copy to Machin, admitting to him that she had failed to write to the brief: 'It was very difficult for me to understand what she wanted . . . I complained to her that I did not much like the idea of writing for an audience of a particular kind. I can't see how one can do that, without losing the force of one's work'.[313] Machin praised the work and its depiction of Botswana,[314] but the response from Simon & Schuster was much less enthusiastic. After several months' delay, Stephenson rejected the book, explaining that, despite her 'high hopes' for the book and the 'great deal of emotion' and 'cast of believable characters', she found it to be marred by 'a confusion of elements that need to be sculpted and polished and crafted into a finished piece of art'. The work was in her view unfinished: 'This is not yet a story, but a dense mine of material

---

[311] Letter, Head to Machin, 19 August 1969, Box B, Folder 60, Item 18, BHP/ KMM.

[312] Letter, Gordon to Head, 28 April 1969, Box A, Folder 24, Item 7, BHP/KMM.

[313] Letter, Head to Machin, 19 August 1969, Box B, Folder 60, Item 18, BHP/ KMM.

[314] Letter, Machin to Head, 2 September 1969, Box B, Folder 60, Item 19, BHP/ KMM.

that you feel strongly but have to articulate and direct. It is still internal'. Her main objection, however, was that the book was unsuitable for young people:

> It does not answer our real concern, which is an honest, contemporary novel about young people, which will expand teenagers' understanding of their own time of life, and of people their own age whose life experience is both dissimilar and analogous. I think you have the seeds for such a book, if you should want to use them ... I hope too, that my frankness does not discourage or hurt you.[315]

Head was indeed discouraged and hurt: she wrote to Machin that she could 'never work with an Anne Stephenson who wants "sculpted art"',[316] and the business relationship with Simon & Schuster came to an abrupt end.

To Head's dismay, she then received further criticism of *Maru* from Bob Gottlieb, her revered editor of *Rain Clouds*. He had recently left Simon & Schuster for Knopf, and Head asked Machin to send him the manuscript as a 'free gift', because he was someone 'on the right wave length'.[317] However, Gottlieb responded that the manuscript was unsuitable for the 'American public'. Baffled, she forwarded his reply to Machin, asking him to 'please analyse this letter':

> What does Bob mean here. Is he really pushing me out of the door, that is, is [*sic*] the contents of MARU so horrific to his delicate white man's taste. I wrote to him, not the American public. I was angry because I thought his letter said: 'I am a white man. I am American society'. He is no fool. He would not in his right mind write that kind of letter to an American

---

[315] Letter, Stephenson to Head, 3 November 1969, Box A, Folder 111, Item 5, BHP/KMM.

[316] Letter, Head to Machin, 10 June 1970, Box B, Folder 60, Item 28, BHP/KMM.

[317] Letter, Head to Machin, 11 February 1970, Box B, Folder 60, Item 27, BHP/KMM.

writer, so I get mad, thinking he's up this pole of 'she's just a black woman so I can shove her out'. That's what it looked like. Was I wrong?

Convinced that Gottlieb would never write 'that kind of letter to an American writer', she concluded that as a 'black woman', he was treating her as a second-class citizen. She continued:

> Nothing hurt me so much as Bob's letter and it seems to me he intended to do this. He'd know me and he'd know that references to the American public would only arouse my contempt, because you don't pander to what the public likes when you swing out against oppression. You are carving a new road. He wrote everything in that letter to cut me dead and throw off any future working partnership. I find this totally unacceptable and cannot for the moment believe all the nonsense he wrote in his letter.[318]

Head was outraged by Gottlieb's suggestion that she should write for the 'American public', and expressed 'contempt' for the idea of pandering 'to what the public likes'. Her attempts to carve out 'a new road' led to unanimous rejection, and she was starting to realise the demands that commercial publishers placed on the African novel.

Gollancz and the Publication of Maru

Maru was in the end rescued by her London editor, Giles Gordon at Victor Gollancz. After the publication of *Rain Clouds*, Gordon had written to Head eagerly anticipating 'novel number 2' and offering to comment on her plans.[319] She sent him the manuscript[320] of what she termed her rather 'dubious love

---

[318] Letter, Head to Machin, 10 June 1970, Box B, Folder 60, Item 28, BHP/KMM.

[319] Letter, Gordon to Head, 24 October 1969, Box A, Folder 24, Item 12, BHP/KMM.

[320] Letter, Head to Machin, 19 August 1969, Box B, Folder 60, Item 18, BHP/KMM.

story',[321] and he replied, praising it for being 'much more perceptive about human beings and what makes them work'. Comparing it with *Rain Clouds*, he judged that her 'prose has a greater inner intensity and perception than it did in places in the earlier book'. Problems began, however, when Gordon sent Head a list of 'comments and suggested alterations' designed to make the book more accessible to 'the British readership of the book'.[322]

Gordon's first recommendation was that Head change the title: 'We all feel here that MARU would not be a good selling title as the name or the word would mean nothing to British readers'. He suggested 'Two Men, Two Women' as an alternative, although he worried that might be a bit hackneyed. He then proposed that the names of four of the main characters be changed to make them simpler and more readily distinguishable for British readers:

> Four of the most important names all begin with M, and at least three of them are in themselves confusing for British readers – Maru, Moleka, Masarwa and Margaret. Would it be possible, and would you agree, to change at least two of these names to words beginning with a letter other than M?

Gordon also advised that the first line of the book be changed, and that the final page, which was dedicated to the British agricultural officer George MacPherson, be deleted as it 'rather spoils what is really the ending'. He recognised that he was treading on delicate ground, for he ended his letter, 'Anxiously, I shall look forward to your reactions'.[323]

Head's response was, as she later acknowledged, 'slightly hysterical'.[324] She emphatically rejected Gordon's changes – 'Giles, I beat down all your suggestions . . . with good reasons' – and insisted that 'I do not write only for white people!!' Regarding the title, she was adamant that no changes be

---

[321] Letter, Head to Gordon, 3 June 1968, Box A, Folder 24, Item 3, BHP/KMM.
[322] Letter, Gordon to Head, 26 January 1970, Box A, Folder 24, Item 13, BHP/KMM.
[323] Ibid.
[324] Letter, Head to Gordon, 19 November 1970, Box A, Folder 24, Item 19, BHP/KMM.

made: 'God help me, it would kill me to change the title. . . . the whole goddam book is MARU and he is a *giant*. Everything I had went into the making of him. Rain Clouds sold on MAKHAYA. MARU will sell 1,000,000 copies. Don't kill that title'. Instead, she cast the responsibility for selling the book back onto Gordon, as the publisher, advising him to 'make the dust jacket POWERFUL'. Head also insisted that the names of the protagonists stay as they were: 'I cannot change the names of Maru, Moleka, Margaret. They mean too much to me and were *carefully* chosen'. Likewise, she emphatically rejected his alteration of the first line of the novel:

> 'The first line . . . 'The rains were so late that year . . . ' I do not like your change to 'The rains were particularly late that year'. I want my lines to stand because they are music and not grammar. There's times music is more important than grammar so I'd like to see 'The rains were so late that year'.[325]

She also refused to let him delete the last page of the novel, writing that MacPherson was 'a *terrific* white man with a heart the shape of the universe itself, therefore page 114 is *for him and cannot be deleted*'.

The only alterations she accepted were Gordon's efforts to 'straighten out' her 'spelling and grammatical errors'.[326] She agreed to change the book's structure to two parts rather than separate chapters and approved his suggestions to delete her 'more extreme Americanisations'. She accepted his advice to tighten her prose 'where it seemed a bit slack and repetitive' and to split her paragraphs up to make for 'easier reading'. Head admitted that Gordon's copy-editing was 'damn good', stating that, 'most of your editing and re-arrangement of sentences, meets with my approval. I call this approval a "wave-length", and we have a good one here'. However, she rejected outright any attempts to make the book more suitable for a British readership: 'I

---

[325] Letter, Head to Gordon, 2 February 1970, Box A, Folder 24, Item 14, BHP/KMM.

[326] Letter, Head to Gordon, 19 November 1970, Box A, Folder 24, Item 19, BHP/KMM.

thought this was my first masterpiece and I was so happy re-reading it. There are passages in it full of wonder'. She rebuked Gordon for trying to make so many changes – 'How can you question my artistic imagination like this? Some things are right according to the story!' – and ended the letter with 'I don't like to get mad, so you must now agree with the parts I corrected'.[327]

In the event, the editing of *Maru* went ahead on Head's terms, and by end of the editing process she jubilantly reported to Machin:

> One thing makes me buoyant though. I have just completed the correction of the proofs of MARU . . . I don't think we will hear the end of it. It will split the skies! I feel it. I really do. I wrote Giles a special letter for perfect editing. It is a terrific job, he did there.[328]

The hardback was published by Gollancz for the British marketplace on 21 January 1971 (Figure 8) to coincide with the publication of the Penguin paperback of *Rain Clouds*, and the rights were thereafter sold internationally. James Currey, former editor of the *The New African* who went on to work as editor for Heinemann Educational Books, bought the rights for the African Writers Series and also bought *When Rain Clouds Gather* for the New Windmill Series, a book series aimed at British schools.[329] Head received an advance of £100 against a royalty of 7.5 per cent for both texts.[330] The book was also published in the United States by McCall in 1971. Reflecting later on the editorial process, Head wrote to Gordon to explain her initial, ferocious response to his suggestions: 'I also want to be free to express myself as I like, and as you know from the work we did on 'MARU' I get slightly hysterical when we don't

---

[327] Letter, Head to Gordon, 2 February 1970, Box A, Folder 24, Item 14, BHP/KMM.

[328] Letter, Head to Machin, 10 June 1970, Box B, Folder 60, Item 28, BHP/KMM.

[329] See Davis, 'A Question of Power', for a discussion of Head's subsequent dealings with James Currey over the publication of her third novel.

[330] Letter, Gordon to Rubinstein, 18 December 1970, Box B, Folder 60, Item 36, BHP/KMM.

Figure 8 Bessie Head, *Maru* (London: Gollancz, 1971), front jacket and spine

see, eye to eye, on eternity'.[331] Thus, by the publication of her second novel, Head had refused to concede to demands to write for a foreign market, successfully asserting her right to artistic freedom and autonomy over her own writing.

[331] Letter, Head to Graham, 19 November 1970, Box A, Folder 24, Item 19, BHP/ KMM.

Conclusion

Bessie Head achieved a remarkable feat in becoming the first 'non-white' female novelist in southern Africa to have her work published. Her career was launched through her connections with the CCF, and she benefited from the support of Randolph Vigne and *The New African*, as well as from publication in *Transition* and *Encounter*. However, she lacked the direct CIA funding and patronage that several of her contemporaries had enjoyed. Rubin writes that some writers were 'mobilised for transnational consumption' by the CCF, while others were denied access to these multiple opportunities.[332] Why Head was denied these opportunities and was relegated to a position on the periphery of the CCF is unclear. Perhaps it was due to her geographical isolation from the main literary centres, what Pascale Casanova describes as the 'aesthetic distance from the place where literary consecration is ordained'.[333] Alternatively, it might have been because she was a female writer, struggling for recognition within the overwhelmingly male literary network of the CCF, or because she was temperamentally ill-suited for the task of cultural diplomacy. Whatever the reasons, it resulted in her becoming reliant on international commercial publishers for her survival as a writer.

Head's interactions with her New York and London literary editors during the publication of her first two novels, *When Rain Clouds Gather* and *Maru*, reveal that she was expected to adapt her work to suit the American and British literary marketplace, to fit genre categories, and to fulfil foreign readers' expectations. The resulting novels, published in hardback in New York and London for an overwhelmingly American and British marketplace display some features of the 'extroverted' African novel. Yet, Head's correspondence with her publishers complicates Julien's interpretation. As a 'displaced outsider', Head regarded herself as geographically and culturally isolated from both her local Botswanan society and her international publishers, and she repeatedly expressed discomfort with the role of a representative and allegorical 'African writer' that was conferred on her by her

---

[332] Rubin, *Archives of Authority*, p. 56.

[333] Casanova, *World Republic of Letters*, p. 23.

American and British publishers and readers. Increasingly, Head refused to cooperate with her editors, and she insisted on the right to tell her own stories, even at the risk of jeopardising her carefully cultivated associations with London and New York publishers.

Conclusion

A Congressional Select Committee was established in 1975, under Senator Frank Church, to investigate 'allegations of abuse and improper activities by the intelligence services of the United States' during the previous two decades.[334] Although there were distinct limits to the degree to which the committee interrogated the work of the CIA,[335] it drew striking conclusions about the extent to which the Agency had co-opted publishers into its covert operation. The committee came to the conclusion that, 'in the world of covert propaganda, book publishing activities have a special place'.[336] It identified that, by the end of 1967, over 1,000 books had been 'produced, subsidized or sponsored by the CIA', many of them through cultural organisations backed by the CIA. Some of these, it discovered, were the result of direct collaboration between the CIA and the author, but in most cases the author was unaware of the CIA involvement.[337] The committee also found that the CIA had infiltrated a number of commercial publishing houses, sometimes without their knowledge, and had formed a 'network of several hundred foreign individuals around the world' which provided the CIA with direct access to 'foreign newspapers and periodicals, scores of press services and news agencies, radio and television stations, commercial book publishers, and other foreign media outlets'.[338] Africa was reported to have been of particular strategic importance in this operation, because of 'the vulnerability of the newly independent nations' to 'communist subversion'.[339] The total cost of this covert propaganda campaign world-wide was estimated at $265 million a year.[340]

The methods adopted by the CIA in this covert strategy in Africa are demonstrated in the case studies in the preceding chapters, from the subsidy of literary magazines and book publishers, to the patronage of authors and editors, and to the funding of TV and radio programmes. There is, however, no evidence of what the Church Report describes as the CIA's 'direct collaboration' with authors and publishers: none of the

---

[334] Church, *Final Report*, p. iii [335] Johnson, 'US Congress and the CIA', p. 496.
[336] Church, *Final Report*, p. 192. [337] Ibid., p. 193. [338] Ibid., p. 192.
[339] Ibid., p. 25. [340] Ibid., p. 193.

recipients of this funding appear to have been aware of its source, and, while the Farfield Foundation attempted to steer *The Classic* in a conservative political direction, it exercised no direct control over the content that was published. The lack of evidence that the CIA recruited African authors and editors in the publication of anti-communist propaganda has led many contemporaries and subsequent historians to deduce that the CIA operation in Africa was apolitical, and that it was a benign form of cultural diplomacy. But this interpretation underestimates the CIA's influence in shaping this sector of African literature. The principal interest of the CIA in the cultural cold war in Africa was in forming an elite association of writers and intellectuals who had close ties to the United States. As the Church Report identified, the CIA's intention was to create a 'network of several hundred foreign individuals around the world' to extend American influence worldwide, as well as to offer these writers direct access to media outlets and book publishers. This is evident in Mphahlele's efforts to build a pan-African community of African writers, in his and Thompson's attempt to develop *The Classic* as a hub for South African writers, and in the CIA's investment in the Transcription Centre as a major centre for diasporic African writers.

The CIA's interventions in the 'restricted field of cultural production' in Africa profoundly altered African literary publishing. Where London was once the centre of publishing for African writers, the Congress for Cultural Freedom supported a new model that was ostensibly small scale and devolved. Literary hubs were funded across the continent – in Ibadan, Nairobi, Kampala, Johannesburg, and Cape Town – for the publication of 'little magazines' and small literary presses, predominantly under African editorship. This appeared to be a radical departure from the colonial literary systems, the 'vertical linkages' of 'power, influence and capital' that Ballantyne describes as radiating from London to the colonial peripheries.[341] Yet, by 1967, it was revealed that this apparently decolonised network of literary publishing had the US government, and specifically the CIA, at its epicentre.

---

[341] Ballantyne, *Webs of Empire*, pp. 16, 15.

Postcolonial African literature was irrevocably changed by these interventions. A privileged group of African writers, predominantly male and highly educated, were hand-picked for star treatment. They were brought into close, dependent relationships with CIA operatives in the Farfield Foundation. Wole Soyinka, Chinua Achebe, Es'kia Mphahlele, Lewis Nkosi, and Kofi Awooner, were, in particular, given international visibility through CIA-funded conferences, festivals, theatre productions, radio programmes, and film and TV broadcasts, and were provided with travel grants and salaries. Their writing was published in the literary magazines supported by the CCF, and the CCF worked closely with British and American commercial publishers to ensure that their work was republished and translated worldwide. Their close associations with America continued after the CCF was closed, and they were awarded professorial positions in American universities. The writers were identified as members of a new canon of postcolonial African writers.

These case studies reveal that, in the cultural cold war in Africa, there were beneficiaries like Wole Soyinka, but there were also outsiders and victims. Writers who were excluded from, or on the periphery of, the CIA network lacked access to this external funding, to publication and promotional advantages, and were obliged to navigate their own literary careers. This involved establishing connections with British and American publishers, but, as the case of Bessie Head demonstrates, meeting the demands of foreign editors, readers, and critics was a process fraught with difficulty. In the case of Nat Nakasa, the interventions of the CIA brought him into direct conflict with the South African state; the plan to use literary magazines to draw South African writers into a wider literary community, closely tied to the United States, was thwarted as black writers were systematically silenced and dispersed by the apartheid government. This led to his relinquishing editorship of *The Classic* and ultimately to becoming an exile in the United States, with tragic consequences.

African literary publishing in the period of decolonisation was, therefore, the site of international power struggles. Many have assumed complicity, even passivity, on the part of African authors and editors in their relationships with their American and British publishers and patrons, but these histories of authorship and publishing reveal that literary production was not a unidirectional process. Instead, African writers frequently resisted attempts to alter their work to suit their foreign patrons, publishers, audiences, or readers. The resulting interactions, confrontations, and negotiations provide an insight into the intertwined networks of power and money underpinning African literary production during the Cold War.

Bibliography

Published Sources

Acott, H., 'Tactics of the Habitat: The Elusive Identity of Nat Nakasa', unpublished MA dissertation (University of South Africa, 2008).

Adejunmobi, M., 'Claiming the Field: Africa and the Space of Indian Ocean Literature', *Callaloo*, 32: 4 (2009), 1247–61.

Amuta, C., *The Theory of African Literature: Implications for Practical Criticism* (London: Zed Books, 1989).

Ashuntantang, J., 'The Publishing and Digital Dissemination of Creative Writing in Cameroon', in C. Davis and D. Johnson (eds.), *The Book in Africa: Critical Debates* (Basingstoke: Palgrave Macmillan, 2015), pp. 245–66.

Askew, K., 'Everyday Poetry from Tanzania: Microcosm of the Newspaper Genre', in D. Peterson, E. Hunter, and S. Newell (eds.), *African Print Cultures: Newspapers and Their Publics in the Twentieth Century* (Ann Arbor: University of Michigan Press, 2016), pp. 179–223.

Athill, D., *Stet: A Memoir* (London: Granta Books, 2000).

Ballantyne, T., *Webs of Empire: Locating New Zealand's Colonial Past* (Vancouver: University of British Columbia Press, 2014).

Barber, K., 'Introduction', in K. Barber (ed.), *Africa's Hidden Histories: Everyday Literacy and Making the Self* (Bloomington: Indiana University Press, 2006), pp. 1–24.

Benson, P., *Black Orpheus, Transition, and Modern Cultural Awakening in Africa* (Berkeley: University of California Press, 1986).

Benson, P., '"Border Operators": Black Orpheus and the Genesis of Modern African Art and Literature', *Research in African Literatures*, 14:4 (1983), 431–73.

Bourdieu, P., *The Field of Cultural Production: Essays on Art and Literature* (Cambridge: Polity Press, 1993).

Brown, R., *Native of Nowhere: The Life of Nat Nakasa* (Auckland Park, South Africa: Jacana, 2013).

Brouillette, S., 'Postcolonial Authorship Revisited', in Raphael Dalleo (ed.), *Bourdieu and Postcolonial Studies* (Liverpool: Liverpool University Press, 2016), pp. 80–101.

Buitenhuis, P., *The Great War of Words: Literature as Propaganda 1914–18 and After* (London: Batsford, 1989).

Bush, R., *Publishing Africa in French: Literary Institutions and Decolonization 1945–1967* (Liverpool: Liverpool University Press, 2016).

Casanova, P., T*he World Republic of Letters* (Cambridge, MA: Harvard University Press, 2007).

Chapman, M. (ed.), *The Drum Decade: Stories from the 1950s* (Scottsville: University of Natal Press, 2001).

Church, F., *Final Report of the Select Committee to Study Governmental Operations with respect to Intelligence Activities*, *United States Senate*, Book 1 (26 April 1976).

Coleman, P., *The Liberal Conspiracy: The Congress for Cultural Freedom and the Struggle for the Mind of Postwar Europe* (New York: Free Press, 1989).

Collings, R., 'The First Commonwealth Arts Festival', *The New African*, 4:7 (1965), 151–2.

Davis, C., 'Creating a Book Empire: Longmans in Africa', in C. Davis and D. Johnson (eds.), *The Book in Africa: Critical Debates* (Basingstoke: Palgrave Macmillan, 2015), pp. 128–52.

Davis, C., *Creating Postcolonial Literature: African Writers and British Publishers* (Basingstoke: Palgrave Macmillan, 2013).

Davis, C., 'Playing the Game? The Publication of Oswald Mtshali', in Raphael Dalleo (ed.), *Bourdieu and Postcolonial Studies* (Liverpool: Liverpool University Press, 2016), pp. 137–158.

Davis, C., 'A Question of Power: Bessie Head and her Publishers', *Journal of Southern African Studies*, 44 (2018), 149–506.

Ehmeir, W., 'Publishing South African Literature in the 1960s', *Research in African Literatures*, 26:1 (1995), 111–31.

Fraser, R., *Book History through Postcolonial Eyes: Rewriting the Script* (London: Routledge, 2008).

Friendly, A., 'Slick African Magazine Gains a Wide Following', *The New York Times* (11 August 1968), 3.

Furniss, G., 'Innovation and Persistence: Literary Circles, New Opportunities, and Continuing Debates in Hausa Literary Production', in K. Barber (ed.), *Africa's Hidden Histories: Everyday Literacy and Making the Self* (Bloomington: Indiana University Press, 2006), pp. 416–34.

Gray, S., *Free-lancers and Literary Biography in South Africa* (Amsterdam: Rodopi, 1999).

Gready, P., 'The Sophiatown Writers of the Fifties: The Unreal Reality of Their World', *Journal of Southern African Studies*, 16:1 (1990), 139–64.

Head, B., 'For Serowe, a Village in Africa', *The New African*, 4:10 (1965), 230.

Head, B., 'A Gentle People', *The New African*, 2:8 (1963), 169–70.

Head, B., 'God and the Underdog: Thoughts on the Rise of Africa', *The New African*, 7:2 (1968), 47–8.

Head, B., 'The Isolation of Boeta L', *The New African*, 3:2 (1964), 28–9.

Head, B., 'Let Me Tell You a Story Now', *The New African*, 1:9 (1962), 8–10.

Head, B., 'Looking for a Rain God: A Story of Botswana', *The New African*, 5:3 (1966), 65.

Head, B., *Maru* (London: Gollancz, 1971).

Head, H., 'Piet de Vries Speaks His Mind', *The New African*, 1:5 (1962), 5–6.

Head, B., 'Snowball: A Story', *The New African*, 3:5 (1964), 100–1.

Head, B., 'Things I Don't Like', *The New African*, 1:7 (1962), 10.

Head, B., *When Rain Clouds Gather* (New York: Simon & Schuster, 1968).

Hench, J., *Books as Weapons: Propaganda, Publishing, and the Battle for Global Markets in the Era of World War II* (Ithaca, NY: Cornell University Press, 2016).

Herdeck, D., *African Authors: A Companion to Black African Writing* (Washington, DC: Black Orpheus Press, 1973).

Hofmeyr, 'Reading Debating/Debating Reading', in K. Barber (ed.), *Africa's Hidden Histories: Everyday Literacy and Making the Self* (Bloomington: Indiana University Press, 2006), pp. 258–77.

Holman, V., 'Carefully Concealed Connections: The Ministry of Information and British Publishing, 1939–1946', *Book History*, 8 (2005), 197–226.

Ibironke, O., *Remapping African Literature: African Histories and Modernities* (Basingstoke: Palgrave, 2018).

Jeyifo, B. (ed.), *Conversations with Wole Soyinka* (Jackson: University Press of Mississippi, 2001).

Johnson, L., 'The U.S. Congress and the CIA: Monitoring the Dark Side of Government', *Legislative Studies Quarterly*, 5:4 (1980), 477–99.

Julien, E., 'The Extroverted African Novel', in F. Moretti (ed.), *The Novel*, vol. 1, *History Geography, and Culture* (Princeton: Princeton University Press, 2006), pp. 667–700.

Julien, E., 'The Extroverted African novel, Revisited: African Novels at Home, in the World', *Journal of African Cultural Studies*, 30:3 (2018), 371–81.

Kalliney, P., 'Modernism, African Literature and the Cold War', *Modern Language Quarterly*, 76:3 (2015), 334–68.

Kalliney, P., *Modernism in a Global Context* (London: Bloomsbury, 2016).

Keany, M., '"I Can Feel My Grin Turn to a Grimace": From the Sophiatown Shebeens to the Streets of Soweto on the Pages of *Drum*, *The Classic*, *New Classic*, and *Staffrider*', unpublished master's dissertation (George Mason University, 2010).

Komey, E. A., 'Wanted: Creative Writers', *West African Review*, 32:407 (1961), 63.

Krishnan, M., *Contingent Canons: African Literature and the Politics of Location* (Cambridge: Cambridge University Press, 2018).

Holt, E. M., '"Bread or Freedom": The Congress for Cultural Freedom, the CIA, and the Arabic Literary Journal *Hiwãr* (1962–67)', *Journal of Arabic Literature*, 44 (2013), 83–102.

La Guma, B. with M. Klammer, *In the Dark with my Dress on Fire: My Life in Cape Town, London, Havana and Home Again* (Auckland Park, South Africa: Jacana, 2010).

Lindfors, B., 'African Literature Criticism and the Post-Colonial Curriculum', *Journal of Literary Studies* 16:3–4 (2000), 5–41.

Lindfors, B., 'Post-War Literature in English by African Writers from South Africa', *The Atlanta University Review of Race and Culture*, 27:1 (1966), 50–62.

Manganyi, C. N., *Exiles and Homecomings: A Biography of Es'kia Mphahlele* (Johannesburg: Ravan, 1983).

Mphahlele, E., 'Mphahlele on the CIA', *Transition*, 34 (December 1967–January 1968), 5–6.

Nakasa, N., 'Comment', *The Classic*, 1:1 (1963), 3–4.

Nakasa, N., 'Comment', *The Classic*, 1:2 (1963), 5.

Nakasa, N., 'Writing in South Africa', *The Classic*, 1:1 (1963), 56–63.

Neogy, R., and T. Hill, 'Liberalism: The Toughest Creed There Is', *Sunday Nation* (11 June 1967), repr. in *Transition*, 75–6 (1997), 312–16.

Ngũgĩ wa Thiong'o, *Birth of a Dream Weaver: A Writer's Awakening* (London: Random House, 2016).

Ngũgĩ wa Thiong'o, *Decolonising the Mind: The Politics of Language in African Literature* (Portsmouth, NH: Heinemann, 1992).

Nkosi, L., 'Review of *The World of Nat Nakasa: Selected Writings* by Essop Patel', *Research in African Literatures*, 9:3 (1978), 475–9.

Nsehe, M., 'The 40 Most Powerful Celebrities in Africa', Forbes, www.forbes.com/sites/mfonobongnsehe/2011/10/12/the-40-most-powerful-celebrities-in-africa (accessed 3 March 2020).

Reuser Jahn, Uta, 'Private Entertainment Magazines and Popular Literature Production in Socialist Tanzania', in D. Peterson, E. Hunter, and S. Newell (eds.), *African Print Cultures: Newspapers and Their Publics in the Twentieth Century* (Ann Arbor: University of Michigan Press, 2016), pp. 224–50.

Rogers, A., 'Culture in Transition: Rajat Neogy's *Transition* (1961–68) and the Decolonization of African Literature', in D. Davies, E. Lombard, and B. Mountford (eds.), *Fighting Words: Fifteen Books that Shaped the Postcolonial World* (New York: Peter Lang, 2017), pp. 183–99.

Rogers, A., 'Officially Autonomous: Anglophone Literary Cultures and the State since 1945', unpublished D.Phil. thesis (University of Oxford, 1914).

Rubin, A. N., *Archives of Authority: Empire, Culture and the Cold War* (Princeton: Princeton University Press, 2012).

Sandwith, C., 'Entering the Territory of Incitement: Oppositionality and Africa South', *Social Dynamics*, 35:1 (2009), 123–36.

Saunders, F. S., *The Cultural Cold War: The CIA and the World of Arts and Letters* (New York: New York Press, 2000).

Saunders, F. S., *Who Paid the Piper? The CIA and the Cultural Cold War* (London: Granta Books, 1999).

Shringarpure, B., *Cold War Assemblages: Decolonisation to Digital* (Abingdon: Routledge, 2019).

Soyinka, W., *You Must Set Forth at Dawn* (New York: Random House, 2007).

Spahr, J., *Du Bois's Telegram: Literary Resistance and State Containment* (Cambridge, MA: Harvard University Press, 2018).

Suhr-Sytsma, N., 'The Extroverted African Novel and Literary Publishing in the 21st Century', *Journal of African Cultural Studies*, 30:3 (2018), 339–355.

Suhr-Sytsma, N., *Poetry, Print and the Making of Postcolonial Literature* (Cambridge: Cambridge University Press, 2017).

Swanepoel, P. C., *Really inside BOSS: A Tale of South Africa's Late Intelligence Service (and Something about the CIA)* (Pretoria: Swanepoel, 2007).

Themba, C., 'The Suit', *The Classic*, 1:1 (1963), 6–16.

Vigne, R., 'Come What May', *The New African*, 5:1 (1966), 1.

Vigne, R., *Gesture of Belonging: Letters of Bessie Head, 1965–1979* (London: SA Writers and Heinemann Educational Books, 1991).

Vigne, R., and J. Currey, *The New African: A History 1962–69* (London: Merlin Press, 2014).

Zimbler, J., 'For Neither Love nor Money: The Place of Political Art in Pierre Bourdieu's Literary Field', *Textual Practice*, 23: 4 (2009), 599–620.

Archival Sources

The Transcription Centre Records, Harry Ransom Centre, University of Texas (TC/HRC)

  1.3 Mbari Writers Conference, Kampala, 1961

  1.5 Berlin Festival, 1964

 11.3 André Deutsch Ltd, 1962–3

 14.7 Cultural Events in Africa, Heinemann, 1964–70

16.11 Achebe, Chinua

16.12 Aidoo, Ama Ata

 17.1 Clark-Bekederemo, J. P.

 17.9 La Guma, Alex

17.17 Neogy, Rajat

17.18 Nkosi, Lewis

17.22 Okigbo, Christopher

17.25 Rive, Richard

17.30 Serumaga, Robert

   18 Soyinka, Wole

 22.2 Cultural Events in Africa, Subscription Records: Correspondence, 1964–72

 23.1 Funding Files, 1961–73: African trip, 1961

 23.2 Farfield Foundation: Correspondence: Platt, Frank, 1965–8

 23.3 Farfield Foundation: Correspondence: Platt, Frank, January 1968–September 1973

 23.4 Farfield Foundation: Correspondence: Thompson, John, January 1963–March 1969

23.6 Stralem, Donald, 1964–73

Wits University Press Special Collections (Wits)

A2696 Nathaniel Nakasa Archive

B1.2 Athol and Sheila Fugard

B1.4 Doris Lessing

B1.5 Arthur Maimane

B1.7 James Matthews

B1.10 Ezekiel Mphahlele

B1.11 Lewis Nkosi

B1.13 Can Themba

B1.14 Other Correspondents

B2 Classic (Miscellaneous)

B2 Black Orpheus (and Transition)

B3.2 Farfield Foundation

Bessie Head Papers, Khama III Memorial Museum, Serowe, Botswana (BHP/KMM)

Box A, Folder 24 Victor Gollancz – Giles Gordon

Box A, Folder 43 Bantam Books – Jean Highland

Box A, Folder 111 Simon & Schuster Inc.

Box B, Folder 60 A. P. Watt Ltd – David Machin, Hilary Rubinstein

Amazwi, South African Museum of Literature, Grahamstown (Amazwi, Grahamstown)

2015.176.1.38 Patrick Cullinan Collection

International Association for Cultural Freedom, Records, Special Collections Research Center, University of Chicago Library (IACF, Chicago)

Box 296, Folder 2 Soyinka, Wole, 1965

Box 377, Folder 6 Soyinka, Wole, 1968–70

Box 518, Folder 10 Soyinka, Wole (University College of Ibadan, Nigeria), 1961–4

Longmans Group Archive, MS 1393, Reading University Library Special Collections (1393, RUL)

Box 285, Folder 22 Beir, U. (ed.) *Black Orpheus*, 1964

Acknowledgments

I would like to acknowledge the support of many friends and colleagues during the writing of this book. In particularly, I thank Samantha Rayner and Bethany Thomas for the opportunity to have this work published as a Cambridge Element, and for their guidance during the publication process. I also would like to thank Beth le Roux and David Johnson for generously reading and commenting on drafts of this work. I have benefited greatly from discussing this project with Shafquat Towheed, Corinne Sandwith and Jane Cockcroft. I also thank James Currey for talking to me about his work on *The New African*, and Tom Holzinger who gave up so much time to reminisce about his friendship with Bessie Head and show me where she lived and worked in Serowe.

I am grateful to my colleagues at Oxford Brookes University for their support, in particular Paul Whitty, Daniela Treveri Gennari and Angus Phillips, who have been unwaveringly encouraging and generous. I also gratefully acknowledge the research funding from Oxford Brookes University, as well as the award of British Academy funding, in the form of a Newton Mobility Grant for the project 'Histories of Publishing under Apartheid'. I also am very thankful for the award of a 2019 Harry Ransom Center Research Fellowship in the Humanities, in the University of Texas at Austin, supported by the Andrew W. Mellon Foundation Research Fellowship Endowment, which enabled me to carry out important research on the activities of the Congress for Cultural Freedom.

A number of people have facilitated the research and writing of this book: Gabriele Mohale was most helpful in enabling me access to the Historic Papers Research Archive at the University of Witwatersrand; Gase Kediseng kindly provided me with access to the Bessie Head Papers at the Khama III Memorial Museum, Serowe; Kate Hayes helped arrange my fellowship at the Harry Ransom Center, while Jim Kuhn provided helpful advice on the archive collections. I also thank Joseph Clayton for his assistance with bibliographic data collection and analysis, and Jacqueline Harvey for her meticulous care in proof-reading the manuscript. I am very grateful to Cambridge University Press's anonymous reviewers for taking the trouble to read and comment on the manuscript, and also to the editorial staff at the press, in particular Annie Toynbee, Emily Cockburn, and Priyanka Durai, for their professionalism in seeing this book into print.

Archival references and quotations are reprinted here with the kind permission of the Historical Papers Research Archive, University of the Witwatersrand, South Africa; the Bessie Head Heritage Trust, Serowe; and the Harry Ransom Center, The University of Texas at Austin. Permission to publish the cover artwork of *Maru* by Bessie Head (London: Gollancz, 1971) has been kindly granted by The Orion Publishing Group.

And my final thanks are to my husband, Andrew Clayton, and my children Joseph, Ellen and Jude, for their constant encouragement.

Publishing and Book Culture

SERIES EDITOR
Samantha Rayner
University College London

Samantha Rayner is a Reader in UCL's Department of Information Studies. She is also Director of UCL's Centre for Publishing, co-Director of the Bloomsbury CHAPTER (Communication History, Authorship, Publishing, Textual Editing and Reading) and co-editor of the Academic Book of the Future BOOC (Book as Open Online Content) with UCL Press.

ASSOCIATE EDITOR
Leah Tether
University of Bristol

Leah Tether is Professor of Medieval Literature and Publishing at the University of Bristol. With an academic background in medieval French and English literature and a professional background in trade publishing, Leah has combined her expertise and developed an international research profile in book and publishing history from manuscript to digital.

About the Series

This series aims to fill the demand for easily accessible, quality texts available for teaching and research in the diverse and dynamic fields of Publishing and Book Culture. Rigorously researched and peer-reviewed Elements will be published under themes, or 'Gatherings'. These Elements should be the first check point for researchers or students working on that area of publishing and book trade history and practice: we hope that, situated so logically at Cambridge University Press, where academic publishing in the UK began, it will develop to create an unrivalled space where these histories and practices can be investigated and preserved.

Publishing and Book Culture

Colonial and Post-Colonial Publishing

Gathering Editor: Caroline Davis
Caroline Davis is Senior Lecturer in the Oxford International
Centre for Publishing at Oxford Brookes University. She is the
author of *Creating Postcolonial Literature: African Writers and
British Publishers* (Palgrave, 2013), the editor of *Print Cultures:
A Reader in Theory and Practice* (Macmillan, 2019) and co-
editor of *The Book in Africa: Critical Debates* (Palgrave, 2015).

ELEMENTS IN THE GATHERING

A full series listing is available at: www.cambrige.org/EPBC

Printed in the United States
By Bookmasters